What People are Saying About Happy Crap

A perfect sequel to Erika's first book, *Happy Crap* helps us identify, move through and replace our damaging self-talk (roof chatter) with reality-based thinking guaranteed to warm our hearts and promptly improve our lives. A real eye-opener, free of psycho-babble and generous with very helpful, practical exercises. Thanks once again, Erika!

> *Drs. Lori & Gregory Boothroyd*
> *authors of* Going Home – A Positive Emotional Guide
> Toward Life-Generating Behaviors

Happy Crap is a treasure trove of practical tools that will help any reader change their Crappy Crap thinking. Erika shares life-changing concepts in an easy to understand format. Happy Crap is the best kind of "crap"!

> *Eric Webster*
> *Coptic Minister*

If you've never had Crappy Crap thinking, then you must be an alien! Erika's practical approach to changing the way we handle our thought process is amazing in its simplicity, but even more amazing in how it can positively impact our productivity, prosperity and peace. Don't miss this chance to change your life for the better … think Happy Crap and discover a happier and much more positive existence.

> *Mary Green*
> *Director Kellogg Community College Lifelong Learning*

D0711325

UNLEASH the POWER of
POSITIVE ASSUMPTIONS

Happy
CRAP

8 TOOLS
to CHOOSE YOUR THOUGHTS for
PROSPERITY, PRODUCTIVITY and PEACE

ERIKA OLIVER

FIRST EDITION

Designed by Andrea Stork & George Foster
Editing by Rachael Bailey, Matthew McCormick & Erik Oliver

Library of Congress Control Number: 2010910809
Oliver, Erika
Happy Crap / by Erika Oliver. 1st ed.

ISBN-13: 978-0-9799025-3-6

1. Happiness. 2. Psychology. 3. Positive Thinking.
4. Communication.

Dedication

Lori Moore is the host of "Mornings with Lori Moore" on WKZO-AM 590 radio in Kalamazoo, Michigan. Lori is admired in the community for her popular show, energetic personality, and community involvement. In December 2008, Lori invited me to talk about an article I'd written called "7 Strategies to Stop Worry."

That was the first day I said, "Happy Crap." Lori really wanted to know how to stop worrying and I said, "Lori, worry is just crap you make up. So, if you are going to make up crap, make up Happy Crap!"

The moment the words "happy" and "crap" left my lips I wondered if I'd gone too far and offended Lori. Lori didn't think so. She laughed her infectious laugh and said, "I love that!"

That was the beginning of Happy Crap. Lori gave me the courage to say it out loud. After that show, I said "Happy Crap" everywhere I went, and it has helped thousands of people realize they have the ability to *choose their thoughts*. I said it often enough to gain the courage to write this book. Thank you, Lori Moore, for not giving me *crap* for saying "Happy Crap!"

Acknowledgements

This book, and every book before and after, is because of and for my husband and two sons. Mark, Erik and Evan, I love you more than ice cream and our special s'mores. Thank you for always "having my back," helping me find my way, and forgiving my crappiness!

Thank you to my friends for long talks, long walks, popcorn and treats. Ronda, Ruth, Diana, Diane, Sheryl, Kathleen, and Brenda you are always with me, in person or in spirit. You are my family.

A special "thank you" to Erik for coming to my rescue by editing, proofreading and brainstorming to make this book the best it could be. Your constant encouragement and telling me, "Mom, if you can't believe in you, then believe in the *me* that believes in you!" kept me going.

Thank you to everyone who has come to one of my talks, read my books, and/or reads my e-newsletter. Your sharing, support and suggestions give me lots of good things to work with. And thank you to the woman buying vegetables at the market today who said, "Tell me some Happy Crap!" All of you make today, and every day, my best day ever!

Contents

Erika's Journey: A Work-in-Progress

At the gym on Wednesday mornings, my husband and I go to a spinning class with a group of class "regulars," the same people each week with one or two variations.

One Wednesday I decided to stay after class and do a few more exercises. Lying on a mat doing crunches I heard women's voices coming from the location of the membership desk. Several of the women in class are friendly and often stay to talk so I thought it was just them. But, the voices seemed loud and there was a lot of laughing.

Was the whole class gathering at the front desk? *Must be everyone but me*, I thought. Crunching and listening, I grew increasingly upset imagining the whole group talking and laughing and *not* noticing I was absent. Worse yet, they were probably *excluding me on purpose* because they didn't like me!

Finally, having had enough of being excluded, I sat up and leaned toward the door to get a good look at the group. What I saw was different than what I expected, and it reminded me how human brains make up crap – nonsense – that causes us to feel really good, or in this case, really bad.

A girls' volleyball team was practicing in the gym. It was their voices I heard, not my classmates talking about me or anything like that. There was no clique or conspiracy to exclude me! It was all in my head.

I share this story with you for two reasons. First, to be honest with you that my journey to optimism is a work-in-progress. Every day I must consciously choose to make up Happy Crap to eliminate the negativity that my mind so easily creates. Secondly, I tell you this story to illustrate how quickly and easily people engage in Crappy Crap thinking and don't even realize it's happening!

After seeing the volleyball team, I laughed and went back to a few more sit ups. I wondered, should I really be writing a book on choosing positive assumptions when I myself am so easily diverted to the negative? Absolutely! If I didn't struggle with negativity, I wouldn't be able to learn the lessons to share with you. Thank you for joining me on this journey – a work-in-progress – from negativity to prosperity, productivity, and peace.

Happy Crap: Unleash the Power of Positive Assumptions

CHAPTER ONE

Happy Crap

The most important lesson I have learned on my journey to optimism is that I am full of crap. Well, maybe not "me" completely, but my thoughts. My thoughts are full of nonsensical, false, and generally useless ideas, most of which are negative!

Scientists, psychologists, and spiritual leaders say that we can choose our thoughts. They also say that the quality of our thoughts – negative or positive – determines the quality of our experiences and our lives. If this is true, why was I choosing so many negative thoughts?

I wanted to have better – more helpful – thoughts that furthered my optimism journey. But, I didn't know where to start – which thoughts to address – or how to go about thinking differently. The "how" of changing my thinking eluded me.

Then I noticed a particular kind of thought that happened often and seemed rather arbitrary. My mind appeared to continuously churn out hypothesis - theories, guesses, assumptions - about people, places, and things. The kind of hypothesis I created also seemed to influence my feelings, conversations, and actions. Just like the experts said!

I was on to something. Particular thoughts – my assumptions - about people, things, or situations impacted how I felt, talked, and acted. If I had a thought such as, *this is going to be hard,* I felt tired, talked (endlessly) about the long and difficult situation, and moved more slowly. On the other hand, if I had a thought of, *I am so excited about the day,* I felt hopeful, talked about the possibilities, and became energetic.

Most of us let our thoughts flow freely without any monitoring, contemplation, or modification. We rarely – if ever – check our thoughts to see if they are accurate or just crap we made up to fill in the missing pieces of a story. By re-crafting some of my thoughts (assumptions), one small story at a time, I have been able to help myself write a whole new life script.

The strategy is called Happy Crap thinking. It is your choice to make assumptions that help you feel happy, experience positive communication, and get the things done that are important to you. Are you ready to learn a powerful, yet simple, strategy to build your best life story? If you are eager to release negative thinking and unleash the power of positive assumptions, you are in the exact right place! Let's change Crappy Crap thinking into Happy Crap thinking for unlimited prosperity, productivity and peace.

Assumptions

Most mornings, my husband and I go through the same routine. He turns off the alarm clock, prepares his work items, sets up the coffee maker, and wakes me up. I put on my exercise clothes, brush my teeth, and collect our water bottles. We drive to the gym.

We assume the alarm will go off, the coffee maker will work, and the car will start. Without assumptions, every day my husband and I would have to reconsider each element of our morning routine.

> **Assumptions are beliefs and thoughts, just crap (nonsense) you make up to fill in the blanks when you don't have all the information.**

Assumptions are beliefs and thoughts, just crap (nonsense) you make up to fill in the blanks when you don't have all the information. You don't know if the past will repeat itself and if people or things will comply with your agenda. The things you believe about your day and the people in it are just thoughts you create to build a story that you use as a map for your day, your week and your life.

Filling in the Blanks

Have you ever read a paragraph with some letters or words intentionally left out? Your brain fills in what it thinks is missing and you derive meaning without having all the facts. Is your interpretation correct? Did you fill in the blanks with the correct letters or words? Sometimes you are correct, sometimes your interpretation is completely wrong, and sometimes your guess is partially true.

It's the same with assumptions. Assumptions fill in the blanks between bits of information when all the facts are unavailable. Together, the available facts and your assumptions form a story, meaning or conclusion. You don't know what your day will bring so you project ahead based on what has happened before and what you wish to have, or believe will, happen in the future. But, just because you have a thought doesn't make it true or accurate.

> **But, just because you have a thought doesn't make it true or accurate.**

Guesses, Not Facts

Assumptions may fill in the blanks where information is missing, but they aren't real, they are guesses. Assumptions, crap you make up, can appear real or seem reasonable (and sometimes they work quite nicely) but that doesn't make them any more true.

Imagine walking out to your car to go to work and discovering a flat tire. How do you feel when you realize that all four tires are not inflated as expected? You might feel surprised because what you *thought* would occur (all four tires fully inflated and your car ready to drive) did not, in fact, happen.

When you assume something, you take it for granted. You believe you know what *will* happen or *is* happening. Part of assuming is assimilating past and current information and deriving a conclusion. Many assumptions appear to be true because they regularly happen, or are based on something that did happen, like our morning routine or having four inflated tires. Routine happenings and past experiences make it easy to confuse assumptions with facts and to believe assumptions *are* facts.

When you believe assumptions to be facts, when they become "real" in your mind, you are shocked when something unexpected happens. If you guess an answer to a question on a test, and you are aware that you are guessing, you become excited if your answer is correct but not really bothered if you are incorrect. You aren't bothered because you know you guessed and the answer may not be correct. But, if you provide an answer that you are certain is correct and it turns out differently, you are surprised and sometimes defensive. You defend an answer because you believe it to be factual.

If you realize assumptions are guesses – *just made up crap* – then outcomes (what actually happens) don't have as big an emotional impact as when you believe your expectations are guaranteed.

Crappy or Happy?

Can you imagine living without assumptions? You would not be able to count on anything in your day! No more taking for granted that traffic lights will work, stores will be open, or your favorite television shows will be broadcast. You would not be able to make plans because there would be nothing to base them on.

Assumptions are the foundation for decisions, goals, and plans. You make daily decisions, set goals, and craft long-term plans using assumptions. Deciding what to have for dinner, setting a weight-loss goal, and making a plan to run for public office are all based on assumptions. Together your smaller assumptions add up to bigger assumptions such as how easy or hard you think life is, what you believe you deserve, and ultimately how much happiness you allow yourself to experience.

Assumptions such as, *Ugh, Monday's are awful,* create a negative base on which everything is built. On the other hand, assumptions such as, *I know it will all work out,* form a positive base from which to craft an optimistic story. It is impossible to build a happy life from a negative base and vice versa. The quality of assumptions, happy or crappy, determines the quality of life.

With People it's Personal

Waking up in the morning, I make assumptions about the clock, coffee maker, and car. I also make assumptions about my husband and two sons. What assumptions do you make? I have found that, for the most part, objects are pretty predictable. People? Not so much!

You don't just live with things, but with people who are also part of your assumptions. When applying assumptions to people, the very nature of complex personal relationships triggers emotion. You don't care what the clock thinks, but you do care what people think – and what they do. Intellectually, you know people cannot be as predictable as things and places, but emotionally, you *think* they can. When people don't follow the course you set for them or follow the assumptions you make about them, you might not feel too happy. When people are involved it feels personal.

"Do you want to meet for breakfast tomorrow?" you ask your friend.

"Sure!" your friend replies.

The next morning you are waiting at the restaurant and it's fifteen minutes past your meeting time. *Where is she? Why is she making* me *wait?* you wonder as your frustration level rises.

You assumed she would be on time and imagined *her* waiting for *you* when you arrived. When you realize your version of "reality" isn't happening, you might think, *she doesn't care enough about me to get here on time*, or *this is going to mess up my whole day waiting for her!*

Your friend arrives and is greeted by your impatient look. She apologizes and shares the story of *her* flat tire. You feel like an ass for assuming she didn't care (remember the saying that assumptions make an "ass" out of "u" and "me"?). Why does it feel harder to make assumptions about people?

Center of the Universe

Assumptions are most challenging with people because people come with their own set of assumptions and throw you off your center. You are literally the physical center of your universe, perceiving and processing everything through your senses. Figuratively, you are the center because you mentally put yourself in the starring role of each story you create with the assumptions you make. It is natural to be the center of your universe. Through awareness you can adjust your perspective, but a starring role will always be the default position for your assumptions.

Each assumption about people or things is really a projection of your feelings and beliefs as the star of your own show. Other people are just supporting actors and actresses and objects are props in the production. Everything is perceived with you at the center.

This would work out fine if it wasn't for those pesky other people. Objects don't have a script, but people do. And, they share the same production while reading from different scripts! Other people don't see you as the center of the universe. They see themselves as the star of the show and you as the supporting performer! This makes creating assumptions about people a bit tricky. Assumptions are necessary to work together, live together, and play together. But, please remember they are *guesses*, not facts.

Tip the Balance to Positive

Guesses will be made and the nature of your guesses (negative or positive) determines how you feel. The nature of your guesses also determines the quality of your relationships and the life choices that are made visible to you. Making positive assumptions didn't, and sometimes still doesn't, come easy for me. When I first started choosing my thoughts, it took me longer to respond in conversations because my default perspective was negative and I didn't have a positive vocabulary. I had to carefully choose my thinking and decide how to express my thoughts. My friends wondered if something was wrong with me when I had less to say and spoke more slowly!

Changing your assumptions may not be easy, or comfortable, at first. But there is great news! All you need to do is tip the balance of your thinking to positive. You don't have to be happy about everything. You can acknowledge that some stuff just sucks. You don't have to give up every negative opinion, criticism or complaint. You simply need to think more positive than negative. The more you tip the balance, the more "results" of happiness you will experience.

Even though a brain churn up so much negative crap, you can easily stop it, by paying more attention to the positives in your life. When something good happens, such as encountering someone you like or having a moment of pride, say it out loud to yourself and others. If you can't or don't want to say it out loud, then just loudly think it by intentionally noticing the positive thought and staying with it for a few minutes. You can only think one thought at a time. If you crowd your brain with positive thoughts, there won't be any room for the negative!

Notice the positive and make more positives by choosing your assumptions. Often it is just as easy – and as "true" – to assume the best as it is to assume the worst. The next time you are driving home from work, assume that your kids, spouse, or significant other has done what you asked and will be so excited to see you. Try assuming meetings will be productive, people will help, and you will easily solve problems.

Tipping the balance to positive happens by taking action to change the patterns of your thinking and your choice of assumptions. You'll find out how to do this by working through a case study called The Susan Story, reading end-of-chapter examples, examining your beliefs and habits, and learning easy Happy Crap thinking tools. Before you know it, you too will be full of crap – Happy Crap, that is!

Spilled Milk: An Example

After finishing a Happy Crap workshop, the conference organizer and I took a walk. On our walk, we were presented with an opportunity to examine our beliefs. Nearing a conference building, we noticed a woman pushing a valet cart down a cobblestone path. The cart, piled high with luggage and groceries, wobbled on the uneven path and threatened to tumble its contents to the ground. The conference organizer rushed to help the woman just as a gallon of milk dropped off the side of the cart and exploded on the walkway.

A man stood to the side and watched making no movement to assist the woman. As we helped, the woman energetically thanked us and said she was worried her husband – the man standing motionless – would try to help. You see, he had had back surgery just a few days earlier and was under strict physician's instructions to not push or lift anything.

After the couple left, I tried to resume our conversation, but the conference organizer stopped me in the middle of a sentence. "I can't believe it!" she said.

"What?" I asked.

"I just assumed that he was being lazy! When I saw her trying to push the heavy cart I was immediately angry at him for not helping her." She went on to share how she planned to chastise him in some way. If the woman hadn't explained the situation, the conference organizer would have treated the man badly because she assumed he was purposely not helping his wife.

It never occurred to me to blame the husband. My assumption was that the wife wanted to push the cart and the husband was graciously letting her take the lead. The same situation, but two different thoughts led to two different stories! The quality of people's assumptions, the crap each of us makes up, create the stories we live.

CHAPTER TWO

Negative Crap

Human beings have, on average, between 40,000 and 60,000 thoughts a day. Of those, 80 percent are negative! When I first read this statistic, I thought, *No way!* because I have been working for years to cultivate my optimism.

If you listened to your thoughts for one day as I suggested in the first chapter, you may have realized – as I did when I listened to mine – that the statistic above is more accurate than you originally believed. When you listen to your thoughts and listen to others speak you notice the insidious nature of negative thoughts. They

Human beings have, on average, between 40,000 and 60,000 thoughts a day. Of those, 80 percent are negative!

sneak into your thinking and tumble out into routine conversation every chance they get!

"She never shows up on time", "He won't answer the phone", and "He always causes an argument at meetings" are statements we think and say without giving them much, or any, consideration. How often do you think or say things such as "The traffic will be horrible" or "This is going to be a long day"?

Believing your guesses are facts is not the most important problem with making assumptions. No, it's the quality of these fabricated thoughts – negative or positive – that has the biggest impact on how you feel. Your relationships and your ability to navigate challenges also depends on the nature of your thoughts.

What Impact Does Negativity Have?

Think again about walking out to your car and discovering a flat tire. What difference does the quality of your thinking make? Eventually the tire will be fixed and you will get to work no matter which path of thinking you choose. The truth is, the quality of your thinking can and does make a difference. Your guesses – the assumptions you make – affect your attitude and your actions which, in turn, affect others' attitudes and actions which then determine how the situation unfolds.

Try this exercise: Play out the scenario of the flat tire for yourself and notice your thoughts. Close your eyes and imagine this happening to you. Do you assume you will be late for work? Do you assume that people will be angry with you? That the service station won't have time to fix the tire? That the whole day will be ruined? At the service station, your negative assumptions cause you to have an attitude that interferes with others' ability and desire to help. If the service station doesn't have time to fix the tire, negative thinking diminishes your capacity to be a creative problem solver. Negative thoughts impair your problem solving and communication skills.

Negative thoughts impair your problem solving and communication skills.

Maybe you assume your co-workers will understand why you are late, the service station people will help and the problem will get solved easily. If you make positive assumptions, what do you think will happen next? Chances are, people will appreciate your positive mood and be more willing to help. Even if the service station doesn't have time to fix your tire, you will be able to find a solution because you believe it's possible. The incident will be a blip on your radar instead of something you complain about all day.

Whichever set of assumptions you make, the quality of your assumptions effectively determines the outcome and impact of the flat tire on your day. This example is a "no-brainer" to choose positive assumptions. So why are so many thoughts negative?

Why So Negative?

Researchers and mental health practitioners are in agreement on the importance of positivity for a successful and happy life. Positive thinking is linked to decreasing depression, improving communication, enhancing creativity, increasing happiness, curing disease, and even losing weight. With all these benefits – and there is proof of the benefits – why do people struggle with positive thinking? Why is it so easy to make up Crappy Crap and sometimes such a challenge to be optimistic?

50/40/10 Theory

One theory, the 50/40/10 Theory, assigns the quality of your thoughts to a combination of three influences: heredity, choice, and experience. Researchers say that 50% of your thinking is due to genetic make-up, 40% is due to your choice of thoughts, and 10% is the result of an external event or circumstance.

> One theory assigns the quality of your thoughts to a combination of three influences: heredity, choice, and experience.

Half (50%) the determining factor of the quality of your thinking is due to genetics. Your parents and their parents were wired to be negative, and they passed the Crappy Crap genes on to you or vice versa, they passed on Happy Crap genes. Family thought patterns are reinforced with negative or positive behavior, along with family routines and customs, which make genetically programmed assumptions your default thought pattern. In other words, faced with any circumstance, you will think like your family does. You will follow your programmed thought pattern until you make a conscious choice and effort, to think differently.

If your thought pattern is negative, it is further reinforced by the social acceptability of whining, complaining, and expecting the worst. Inheritance of negativity can make choosing positive assumptions difficult because you must make an effort to notice your thoughts and take action to change them. This process is usually slow, and is done one thought at a time.

Choice influences 40% of your thinking. No matter what your upbringing or present situation, you have ample choice about how you want to think about a person, place or thing.

Michael J. Fox, was a popular actor in the 1980's. Almost twenty years ago he was diagnosed with Parkinson's disease. Instead of staying home he went to the ancient Kingdom of Bhutan in the Himalayan mountains South of Tibet. In Bhutan, Fox studied the country's philosophy of Gross National Happiness. According to the philosophy, the happiness of the people precedes even the Gross National Product. After visiting Bhutan, Fox said, "Your happiness grows in direct proportion to your acceptance, and in inverse proportion to your expectations." In other words, what you expect, and the assumptions you choose, decide your level of happiness.

If you were raised in a pessimistic family and are experiencing a sad, scary, or serious event, the 50/40/10 Theory suggests a significant opportunity to choose how you think and what you believe. You have plenty of room to choose to assume the best. The opposite is also true, raised in an optimistic family and experiencing a positive, pleasurable, or prosperous event, you have plenty of room to choose to assume the worst.

The final factor influencing your thinking is circumstance. Your situation, or the event you are experiencing, influences 10% of your thinking. This is amazing to me! How often do I blame how I am feeling on an event? I feel bad because my friend was late to breakfast, my tire is flat, or my son barked at me after school. Whatever the event, it actually plays a minuscule role in your level of optimism.

Situations and events, although often held accountable for feelings, have very little to do with whether you think positive or negative thoughts. Genetics and choice have the greatest influence over how you think.

Brain Chemistry

Other research presents the important role of brain chemicals on your level of optimism. Neurotransmitters, chemicals that send information from one cell to another, (and some brain proteins) shape mood, influence mental health, and impact the quality of thinking. One study discovered brain circuitry for some neurotransmitters is a shared pathway leading to the amygdala, an almond-shaped mass of gray matter deep inside the brain, which regulates emotion. When a pathway is shared, only *one* circuit, positive or negative, can be triggered at a time.

Your personal chemistry impacts your natural response and, maybe, how easy or difficult it is for you to choose your thinking. Everyone's brain chemistry is different and can be influenced by many factors. For example, stress, illness, injury, genetic make-up, medications, and exposure to trauma can all alter brain chemistry. Brain chemistry can also be changed in a positive way by eliminating harmful influences, engaging in psychotherapy, and using traditional and/or holistic medicinal approaches.

Negativity Spreads

Negativity is contagious and it's everywhere! Just as viruses and bacterium are spread when someone shares germs in public, negativity is spread when someone shares pessimistic thoughts in public or private. It is difficult to stay resistant to negativity with large or prolonged amounts of exposure to Crappy Crap.

Negative thoughts are also picked up from what you listen to, watch, and read.

Negative thoughts are also picked up from what you listen to, watch, and read. Then you spread it and pick up more Crappy Crap by complaining, gossiping, and sharing negative stories.

Spreading negativity is a form of socialization, and is culturally encouraged, even for optimistic people. You probably encounter people many times each day who are eager to share something sad from the nightly news, or some other negative gossip.

"Did you hear that the economic crisis is going to get worse?" remarks the exercise instructor to the class. "The wife of a guy at work left him and took all his money," says a neighbor. And, so it goes on and on, story after story. When I stopped watching television news ten years ago, I was concerned I might miss important information. There was nothing to worry about, as there is no shortage of people willing to share bad news!

Negativity spreads just like disease and it's catching. So, cover your mouth and your ears when you encounter pessimism.

Crap Happens

Life presents many challenges, but negative assumptions erect barriers that prevent you from seeing possibilities, taking responsibility and choosing positive action to overcome challenges. Challenges happen daily in the form of traffic jams, personal and work-related misunderstandings, occasional illness and business mistakes, and with unexpected instances of death or broken relationships.

Challenges – the crap of life – may trip you up, but it's negative assumptions that stop you. Crap and life happen. If you let it,

> **Challenges — the crap of life — may trip you up, but it's negative assumptions that stop you.**

negativity also happens. You don't have control over many events, and you certainly don't have control over other people, but you *do* have control over what you think. Even if you are not wired for positivity, have chemical imbalances, or are infected by the negativity of those around you, a choice remains. You can *choose* to magnify the good and shrink the bad. You can choose to make positive assumptions – to tip the balance – and unleash your power.

Choosing positivity does not mean "bad" or challenging things won't happen, but it does mean the crap will have less of an impact, visit less frequently, and when it does come, it won't stay around as long. With your ability to choose positive assumptions, you can overcome a predisposition to negativity and successfully navigate challenging events. My personal wiring is strung negatively. I've experienced trauma and been infected by many negative people, but I have been able to leverage my choice and tip the balance to positive.

If you want to choose different thoughts, just how do you do it? I have tried many things to improve my happiness and all have worked to some degree, but nothing has had the impact and staying power of choosing positive assumptions. Once I figured out the Happy Crap method for choosing positive assumptions, all the other things (healthy eating, exercise, therapy, positive people) worked better!

So you now understand how assumptions work and why negativity is often the default thinking pattern. What's next? We'll find out how to choose positive assumptions by transporting ourselves through The Susan Story in the next two chapters and learn a 3-step process to Happy Crap thinking.

The Perfect Game: An Example

As I am writing this, the newspapers and television news are full of the story of the "almost perfect" baseball game. Detroit Tigers pitcher, Armando Galarraga, had 26 consecutive outs with no one on base in a game against the Cleveland Indians. One more out and he would have pitched the perfect game that has only been done 20 times before in the history of major league baseball. It was a great moment for the Tigers and for Galarraga who was brought up from the minors just a few years ago.

On the last out, when everyone thought the perfect game was had, the first base umpire, Jim Joyce, called the Cleveland Indians' player *safe* at first base. Everyone at the game and watching on television knew the player was out. Upon review, the call was clearly a mistake. Baseball rules forbid changing a call so the umpire's decision would stand.

Joyce could have made excuses, but he didn't. Armando Galarraga could have thrown a fit, but he didn't. In fact, this was the perfect game to display "bad" behavior from either man. Most people expected the ball player to be mad, even outraged, and act out. And, most people expected the umpire to make excuses and blame others.

Both men made a *choice* to accept the situation, accept their role, and believe that all would work out as it should. Maybe they were raised to take responsibility for their actions and be gracious, but this situation was a magnificent test of anyone's inherited or learned positivity. I don't know if I would have acted graciously or acknowledged full responsibility, but they did. They exercised all 40% of their choice.

It worked out! Each was acknowledged and rewarded in different ways. Even though the game wasn't recorded as a perfect game, it will be remembered as perfect in other ways.

Whatever your situation, upbringing, or personal history you can also choose to play a truly perfect game in life.

CHAPTER THREE

The Susan Story: Crappy Crap

The Susan Story is a composite of real life events. The name "Susan" represents a conglomerate of different people with whom I have worked and who I have observed. There is a little bit of all of us in The Susan Story.

Susan Leaves

Imagine you are at work. Along with the rest of your team, you've been

> **There is a little bit of all of us in The Susan Story.**

working overtime for the last six weeks. While you normally arrive at 8:00 a.m. and leave at 4:00 p.m., a special project with a tight deadline and a less than optimal number of people has your team staying an average of two extra hours each night. You have not been home before 6:30 p.m. in weeks. You are tired.

It's 4:00 p.m., you wish you could leave, but to remain on schedule you will need to do two solid hours of work before going home for the night. *I'd rather be home, but I'm not the only one who is tired*, is your thought as you decide to take a break before tackling the final stretch of the day.

Making your way to the break room, you leave your work area and walk down a hallway. Passing a large window facing the employee parking lot, you glance out of the window and notice Susan, one of your team members, walking toward her car.

Susan has her coat draped over her left arm, her purse slung over her right shoulder, and in her right hand she carries a workbag that was a birthday present from the team.

You watch as Susan switches her workbag to her left hand and with her right hand, opens the car door. She climbs inside her car, shuts the door, the reverse lights illuminate, and she backs out of the parking space and drives away. The clock's hands are just past 4:00 p.m.

What Are You Thinking?

When you left your workspace to take a break you wished you were done for the day, but you also acknowledged the efforts of your team members and the importance of the work. After watching Susan leave, are you still thinking about being part of a team effort and the importance of your work or are you wondering where Susan is going?

As you watch Susan, do any of these thoughts cross your mind?
- Where does she think she is going?
- Why does she get to go home?
- Slacker!

- Maybe her child has a baseball game.
- My child has a baseball game and I'm still here!
- She ditched us!
- I work so hard and I never get a break.
- It's not fair that Susan gets to leave and I don't!

What Are You Feeling?

Before taking a break and seeing Susan, you felt a bit tired, but not unhappy. Do you still feel optimistic about the next two hours of work? Are you focusing on the strength and dedication of your team members?

After seeing Susan leave, are you feeling any of these emotions?

- Anger
- Confusion
- Abandonment
- Irritation
- Frustration
- Resentment

Creating a Story

Standing by the window watching Susan, you make script changes based on what you see, what you think is happening, and how you feel. As you rewrite your story you realize you still have work to do and remember you were on your way to get coffee. Taking your eyes off Susan's empty parking space, you continue down the hall to the break room. While replaying the scene of Susan leaving the building, you pour yourself a cup of coffee and continue to develop your new story. Is your story positive or negative?

Spreading the Crap

With your coffee mug full, you make your way back to your desk. Thinking about Susan, you don't notice where you are walking and run right into Mike, another co-worker on your team. Luckily, you don't spill your coffee on Mike. When you apologize, he asks where you are going in such a hurry.

What do you say to Mike? Do you smile, express your enthusiasm to get back to work and ask how his portion of the project is coming along? Maybe. Most likely you let him know that *Susan* has left the building.

What does Mike say? He may vouch for Susan's character, but it's more likely he will add to your story by sharing some additional "information" about Susan. Your conversation might go something like this:

"Susan went home!" you share.

"Really? I'm not surprised. Last week she turned a report in late," offers Mike.

"No one seems to do as much work as us," you add.

"I agree – especially not Susan!" replies Mike.

You didn't spill coffee on Mike, but you did get some crap on him. Just as you will take the Crappy Crap thinking back to your desk, Mike will carry it with him and probably keep the negativity going.

After talking with Mike, you continue to your desk. What are the chances you will be able to completely concentrate on your work? Are you able to think about Susan for only one minute and then decide it's not your concern? Or, do you think about what you will say when you see Susan next or craft a plan to make her exit known to the boss?

Thinking negatively about Susan's leaving, sharing it with a co-worker who adds to it, and adding your own detail and supporting information makes for a Crappy Crap story. As you continue to think about Susan, focusing on your work is nearly impossible. What do you do for the next two hours?

Here are some options – I've done them all – upon returning to your desk!

- Write hate e-mail to Susan and send a copy to the Department Manager.
- Surf the Internet for stories of other slacker co-workers.
- Call another co-worker to ask if they know that Susan left.
- Call home to alert your family members of the unfairness at work.

Aside from not getting work done, what else happens when you create a negative version of The Susan Story? How do you feel? Who and what else is affected?

Chances are you don't feel good about how you spent the last two hours at work, you might feel angry about not accomplishing all you had planned, and you might even blame Susan.

When you arrive home, your family members are waiting with dinner. Do you greet them warmly? Or does the story of Susan's leaving become *your* story as you effectively share your negativity with your family?

You hold onto your story so tightly that it affects every conversation that evening. Your voice retains an angry tone and your responses become sarcastic. In bed, you lie awake and continue to stew over the day's events, imagining what you want to say to Susan. With little sleep, the next morning you blow off going to the gym and skip a healthy breakfast to get to work early and catch up. At your desk, you finally manage to forget about Susan and concentrate on your work. Then, into your office walks Susan!

Assumptions Become Reality

"I'm so glad you are here," Susan says desperately as she enters your office. "I really need your help with a portion of my project that is due by noon. Will you help me?"

You keep a pleasant look on your face, although on the inside your lips curl like the Grinch as he imagines destroying Christmas for all the Whos in Whoville.

"Susan, that sounds important," you say, faking concern. "I truly *wish* I could help you, but I have a deadline that can't be changed."

Susan hears and feels the contempt in your voice and is confused by your underlying anger and lack of support. She leaves your work area and on her way back to her desk runs into your co-worker, Mike.

"Mike, what's wrong with her?" says Susan, pointing to your office.

"You know how touchy she is," replies Mike. "She wants all the glory for herself. Just last week I asked for her help and she gave me some lame excuse. She's definitely not a team player."

"That's the last time I ask for her help!" Susan angrily responds, "And if she thinks I'm going to cover for her vacation, she's crazy."

How many relationships have been affected by one negative assumption about Susan leaving work at 4:00 p.m.? Obviously, your relationships with Susan, Mike, your family and yourself have been impacted. How might your assumptions – the made-up nonsense – affect the rest of the team, clients, friends, neighbors, extended family or even your pets? Negative assumptions about Susan's leaving are turning into negative realities.

Negative assumptions about Susan's leaving are turning into negative realities.

New Training Program: An Example

A Human Resources Manager planned a series of on-line classes to replace the current classroom instruction for employee development. She was excited about the comprehensive material, quality instruction, on-line convenience, and the cost savings. With all of the positive attributes of this change, the Human Resources Manager still insisted the employees would not like the new program because classes would need to be completed outside of work time.

"How do you know they won't like the format?" I asked.

"I just know they won't be happy and participation will be low," she confidently explained. She went on to offer her ideas and assumptions about why this would be true. In her version of the story, the employees expected all training to be done on company time and they would not be able to see the improvements or the opportunities presented because their principle concern would be completing the course work outside of business hours. The company had never tried this before and the employees did not know about the new program so all of her assumptions truly were guesses.

"There's no way anyone will agree to take classes on personal time," she insisted.

"I can guarantee they won't like it," I said.

"Really? How do you know?" she replied.

"I don't know, but *you* know," I stated.

The employees will hear her reservations about the program and will believe the format is inconvenient because, well, the *manager* believes that. She will effectively transfer her belief that they won't be happy and that assumption will become a reality.

On a more optimistic note, the opposite could also happen. She could share her enthusiasm for the benefits and simply state the facts, focusing the balance of her energy on the positive aspects of the new training. Chances are people will see the benefits and share her enthusiasm. When the Human Resource Manager "looked out of the window," she formulated a negative story and that story will stick to if she doesn't change her thinking.

CHAPTER FOUR

The Susan Story: Happy Crap

When you see Susan walk to her car, memories and beliefs are triggered before you even realize what's going on. Your mind instantly uses the memories and beliefs to fill in the blanks to form a story. The first indication that your thoughts are negative or positive is physical. If your body feels relaxed – you feel happy or have a neutral feeling – you can bet you are creating a positive story. If you feel tension in your body, listen for negative thinking. If you want to change your thinking, this is the moment of choice.

> **The first indication that your thoughts are negative or positive is physical.**

3 Steps to Happy Crap

How do you stop the downward spiral of Crappy Crap thinking? Simple, you replace your negative story, with positive assumptions using the following three steps:

Step 1: Identify the FACTS

Step 2: Acknowledge your ASSUMPTIONS

Step 3: Fill in the blanks with HAPPY CRAP

Taking a moment – and that is all it takes – to identify the facts tells you what you really know *for sure* about a situation. Most likely you will find that you know very little. Everything that is not a fact is a thought you constructed, it's just crap you made up!

You have no control over the facts, but you do have 100 percent control over your assumptions. Knowing the facts, you are able to identify all of your other thoughts as assumptions you created to fill in the blanks of the story. Any thought that is not a fact is an assumption and any assumption can be changed.

> **You have no control over the facts, but you do have 100 percent control over your assumptions.**

Now you can replace any assumptions that don't serve you. Since assumptions are just crap you make up, you are free to create assumptions that give you energy and help you achieve prosperity, productivity and peace.

Let's work through each of the steps using The Susan Story so you can practice making up Happy Crap.

Step 1: Identify the Facts

The story you created about Susan came from facts plus the assumptions your mind made up. You filled in the blanks by adding to what you actually saw. If you want to choose a different story, the first step is to list the facts and *only* the facts. What do you know for sure about Susan's leaving?

FACTS:
- Susan is walking toward her car.
- It is 4:00 p.m.
- She has her coat, purse and workbag.
- Susan gets in her car, backs out of her space, and drives out of the parking lot.

When you look at the facts of Susan's leaving, you realize you don't have enough information to support negative feelings, a negative story, or any story!

Step 2: Acknowledge Your Assumptions

The next step is to list your assumptions, or the crap you made up. Think about what you imagined you would say to Mike or to your family members and make a list of your assumptions. You can draw an imaginary thought bubble over your head and fill in your thoughts about Susan. Or, you can just make a list.

What are the assumptions you made about Susan? The most common assumption is that Susan went *home*. When you look at the facts, you realize that you have no idea where Susan went. The possibilities about where she could be going are endless.

Omitting some of the more "colorful" words people have used when completing The Susan Story, here are some assumptions that others have made about Susan's leaving:

- Susan went home.
- Susan left unfinished work for others to complete.
- She receives special attention that no one else gets.
- Susan had a doctor's appointment.
- Susan ditched the team and now the project won't get done on time.
- Susan's child was sick.

Consider the following chart of facts and assumptions. It is so easy to add or delete words and create a meaning or a situation that does not exist!

Fact	Assumption
Susan left at 4:00 p.m.	Susan went *home* at 4:00 p.m.
Susan didn't tell me where she is going.	Susan *doesn't want me to know* where she is going.
Susan is not here doing her work.	Susan *didn't finish* her work.

Step 3: Fill the Blanks with Happy Crap

Once you identify the difference between the facts and your assumptions, the final step is to substitute Happy Crap thinking for any unhelpful negative assumptions. Starting with the facts, you make up a story about Susan's leaving – or whatever your situation may be – that is *positive*. The more outrageously positive your story, the better!

This is so simple, but not always easy. For some reason, it is more comfortable to assume the worst instead of the best. Imagine Susan leaving for a reason that will help the team. Is that hard to imagine? With a little practice, making up Happy Crap becomes easier, feels good, and creates a positive reality. It's okay if what you initially make up isn't true!

Happy Crap Walk-Through

Take a deep breath and review the facts. In this situation, what do you know *for sure*? You see Susan leaving the building and the parking lot, she has her things with her, and the clock shows 4:00 p.m. Next, identify your assumptions. Whatever is not a fact is an assumption. Do your thoughts make you feel good? If they don't make you feel good, replace the Crappy Crap thinking with Happy Crap. How do you do that?

Start by making a list of the *most* positive reasons that Susan might be leaving. Remember, it doesn't matter where Susan is actually going. What matters is where you *think* she is going and the "reality" or truth of the situation is not your concern (or may not be available) in this step.

There are two important parts to this step. First, use your imagination to push the limits to create the most positive, even outrageous, explanation for Susan's leaving. This might be a challenge because the cultural belief – and probably your personal belief – is that you should be "realistic." Cognitive behavioral therapy asks people to replace negative thoughts with realistic positive alternatives. My experience is that I need a little momentum to propel me out of a negative rut. An "extreme" positive assumption is just a force to push past a negative story.

Second, be sure your reasons are truly positive. A reason may sound good and seem positive, but when you review it, it's really not. Think creatively and carefully. Your instructions are to create the most positive assumptions for Susan to be leaving work before everyone else.

Now list at least ten *outrageously positive* reasons that Susan is leaving work at 4:00 p.m. If you get stuck before you reach ten reasons, flip through a magazine to get ideas or ask someone to help you brainstorm. Do what you need to do in order to complete the list.

10 Outrageously Positive Reasons

1. _____

2. _____

3. _____

4. _____

5. _____

6. _____

7. _____

8. _____

9. _____

10. _____

Were you able to be creative? How do you feel? When people make a list of outrageously positive reasons for Susan leaving work at 4:00 p.m., some struggle with pushing past "usual" reasons and adhering to the "most positive" rule. "Susan had to take her son to a doctor's appointment," some say. They are staying in the safe realm of realistic possibilities and not venturing into the *most positive*. How positive is a doctor's appointment?

Some people take on the assignment with great enthusiasm and push the limits of creativity. "Susan has found the cure for cancer in her spare time and is going to a press conference to announce this breakthrough finding," said one very creative person.

Here is a sample list of positive assumptions others have made up:

- Susan won the lottery and has left to collect her winnings, which she is sharing with all of us.
- Susan's daughter had a baby and she is a new grandmother.
- Susan has landed a new account for our company that will allow us to hire more employees.
- Susan has ordered, paid for, and is picking up food for all of us.
- Susan has a meeting with the Executive Committee to secure raises for all of us.
- Susan is meeting with someone to gain information that will complete the project several weeks ahead of schedule.
- Susan is preparing a surprise party for me because I am her favorite co-worker.
- Susan is picking up season football tickets for me to see my favorite team.
- Susan came in early and has actually worked more hours than any of us.
- Susan is celebrating her wedding anniversary.

Do any of your assumptions match those on this list? Was the process fun and easy or uncomfortable and challenging? If you continue to make up Happy Crap, it will get easier and more fun. Happy Crap thinking can become your "imaginary friend" that supports you and builds a positive reality.

Where is Susan Really Going?

But, where is Susan really going? When will you know? Maybe tomorrow, maybe never, or maybe you don't need to know. The most important aspect of this exercise is not wether you know the "truth" about Susan's departure, but how your thinking about the situation makes you feel.

When you fill in the blanks of the story with Happy Crap, you will feel better, you will have better relationships, and accomplish more. Also, it has been my experience that choosing a positive vantage point positions you to hear the "real" story about Susan because your positive approach makes you a trusted, valuable member of the team.

Negative assumptions are no truer than the positive assumptions you create. When you think about the positive possibilities of Susan's leaving, how do you feel? Any of the Happy Crap thoughts, positive assumptions you make up, will have a constructive effect on you and those around you. Thoughts don't have to be true to have an impact. It doesn't matter *where* Susan is going, or if you ever know the real story.

Unleash the Power of Positive Assumptions

Now replay The Susan Story inserting a Happy Crap assumption. Standing at the window watching Susan leave, you feel yourself tense up and realize you are making up Crappy Crap.

A quick review of the facts uncovers that you know very little about Susan's leaving and most of your thoughts are assumptions.

You realize you don't know if Susan is going home. It doesn't really matter where she is going. It is, after all, *Susan's* story, not yours. You decide to choose a positive assumption to replace your negative thoughts. Because you really want to end the extra hours at work, you decide Susan is going to speak with the Senior Management Team to secure more staff along with bonuses for everyone. Now you'll be able to take that vacation in Europe!

With this positive thought about Susan, you get your coffee and discover Mike walking down the hall. This time you are not distracted by negative thoughts and don't bump into him. Do you complain to Mike about Susan? Probably not. There is nothing to complain about. You greet Mike with a smile and ask how his portion of the project is progressing.

Back at your desk, you realize that Susan's exit has nothing to do with you directly and it is easy to focus on your work. You may think about Susan's leaving for a moment, but only to laugh at the creative assumptions you made up. The next two hours fly by as you accomplish your work.

At home, you are glad to see your family. You relax at the dinner table as you actively listen to your family talk about their day. Sleeping well, you go to the gym the next morning and enjoy a healthy breakfast. You arrive at work ready to finish the project.

As you're working at your desk, Susan steps into your office. Her portion of the project hit a snag and she needs your help right away. Thinking about the Happy Crap you made up the previous day, you smile at Susan and gladly help her.

When Susan leaves your office, she sees Mike in the hall. "She is always so helpful!" remarks Susan to Mike. Mike agrees.

Could it really be that simple? Yes! Think back to a recent conflict and ask yourself, *What did I make up*? You may wonder, *What about what the other person made up*? The *only* story you have control over is your own and it only takes one person – you – to stop the negativity!

After conducting this exercise with groups, I notice a change in energy. People laugh, move around, smile and are eager to share when they make up Happy Crap. It is a very different feeling from the time they shared their first thoughts about Susan leaving!

Caribbean Vacation: An Example

About a year ago I wrote a proposal for a client with whom I really wanted to work. We were the perfect fit. The team's challenges were in my area of expertise, the leader shared my positive approach philosophies, and the team members were open to a new way of working.

We discussed the particulars of the project and then, I sent the proposal and told them I would call the next week to follow up. I made one phone call and left a message. She did not respond. After a couple of days, I sent an e-mail. It is not unusual to misplace a phone message so I wasn't concerned at all. There was no response to the e-mail.

That happens, I thought imagining technical difficulties with her e-mail system. I placed one more call and, greeted by the answering machine, left another message. Several days passed and still no response. I began to think up stories about why she hadn't called. My brain filled in with assumptions where the facts left off.

Sitting in my car at a stoplight, I noticed tension in my back and my shoulders creeping up toward my ears. Realizing I was making up Crappy Crap, I immediately took the steps to replace my negative assumptions with Happy Crap.

First, I listed the facts:

- The proposal was sent on time.
- Two phone messages were left.
- One e-mail was sent.

Even though I racked my brain, there were no other facts. The truth was I simply didn't know anything else.

What am I assuming? I asked myself. Here are the thoughts I was making up:

- I made a big mistake in the proposal and she is too angry to even talk to me.
- They found someone better.
- They decided I don't have enough experience to handle this job.
- She just doesn't like me.

I was in deep – making up crap – so I made a conscious decision to replace the Crappy Crap thoughts with Happy Crap. The new story I created for myself was as follows:

My potential client had been working so hard that the company rewarded her with an all-expenses-paid trip to the

Caribbean for her and her family. She had to leave quickly and wasn't able to call me. In fact, at that *very* moment she was on an island and has just remembered she was supposed to call. Since she didn't have phone service, she found a local jewelry merchant and bought several pieces of beautiful silver jewelry she knew I would love. As she bought the jewelry, she thought about how much she was looking forward to working with me.

I knew this story wasn't real, but it made me happy! I smiled, my shoulders returned to their normal position and my face relaxed. In fact, those few minutes of "day-dreaming" caused me to put the whole thing aside and just trust that whatever the outcome of the proposal, it would be the best for me and this company.

When she called three days later, she apologized for the delay and explained that auditors had unexpectedly arrived, tying up 100 percent of her time. She accepted the proposal as written and made a date to begin our work.

What might have happened if the Crappy Crap thoughts had been allowed to continue? I might have tried to contact her again, possibly coming across as pushy or disrupting her concentration on the audit. My anxiety might have shown in my voice and made her doubt her choice. I could have taken my fear and insecurity into the assignment and not felt free to do my best work.

Those are just some possible outcomes with that client. What about my relationships and concentration with other clients? How about my happiness and focus at home? With friends? Taking just a few minutes to notice negative thoughts and replace them with Happy Crap thinking changes how you feel and crafts your story's – happy or unhappy – ending.

CHAPTER FIVE

Your Story: Happy or Crappy?

Who was the main actor, the star, in The Susan Story? If you said "Susan", think again. Your mind made assumptions about where Susan was going in reference to *you* and how Susan's leaving the office would affect *you*. The Susan Story is a great example of how we all create stories with ourselves as the principal actor. But more important than who you cast in the starring role is what kind of story you create. Do you create mostly tragedies with you as the victim, dramas with you at the center of turmoil, or adventures with you as the hero? You are the star, and also the writer, producer, and director of each and every chapter in your life story. Is your story happy or crappy?

Take yourself back to the window and watch Susan walk to her car, get in, and drive away. Why did you assume Susan's leaving would have any impact on you?

Perhaps while watching Susan leave, an old story was triggered. If you had a previous experience with a co-worker who left the work for others to complete, but somehow received all the recognition, you may react to Susan's departure without realizing you're burdening Susan with your past experiences and subsequent beliefs. The Susan Story becomes part of an old, outdated story.

Susan's leaving didn't have anything to do with you, you added yourself to the mix. Suddenly Susan has left *you*, created more work for *you*, become the cause of *you* missing your child's sporting event.

> **Susan's leaving didn't have anything to do with you, you added yourself to the mix.**

If Susan's leaving validates some of your negative beliefs or reinforces doubts about yourself, then her leaving is incorporated as proof that "life is unfair" or "I have to do all the work." Maybe Susan's leaving validates *your* story that you work harder than others. Sometimes others' failings or choices are viewed as proof of your own superiority.

Whatever title you give your story, negative or positive feelings – as well as negative or positive assumptions – all come from your belief system. If you are feeling unappreciated at work or guilty for not attending your child's sports or school event, your feelings and beliefs determine how you write The Susan Story.

Understanding you are the center of your universe, knowing the benefits of positivity, and wanting to change your thinking won't be enough until you confront the beliefs – accepted thoughts behind your thinking – that underlie your assumptions.

Old Reels

Assumptions come from beliefs which are passed down from family members or acquired through life experiences. Beliefs are old reels that may or may not continue to be accurate. Either way, many beliefs become habits. When something happens to you in one circumstance, you create a belief and apply it to similar situations. Old reels have opening lines such as *I knew that was going to happen*, or *Every time I do that the same thing happens*, or *I know exactly what he will do.*

If you had only positive experiences with co-workers in the past, you might not have noticed Susan was leaving or given it a second thought. So, a person with positive parents and mostly positive experiences makes positive assumptions most of the time? Unfortunately, the quality of your assumptions (the content of your story) does not solely rely on your personal experiences. Any contact with others' negative experiences or beliefs, including cultural beliefs, can influence your thinking and become part of your old and new reels.

Reading about the unemployment rate, hearing your child's friend talk about his or her parent missing the big game, or listening to a co-worker complain about not being recognized – and tens of thousands of other potential contacts with negative thinking can – and *will* – impact your beliefs and consequently affect your assumptions. Whether beliefs flow from your own experiences or influences outside of you, they can be changed a just like thoughts can be changed. The first step is to recognize the beliefs you have about others and yourself.

Your Own Crap: What You Believe about Others

You make more judgments about other people and how things should be than you are aware of and would probably want to admit. Some are general, (about a group of people such as nurses, teenage boys, or professional sports players) and for the most part harmless. Other judgments – more personal – have the potential to cut deeper, such as beliefs about neighbors, family members, and co-workers.

Here's an exercise that may help you become more aware of negative or positive beliefs about *others* which you may have unwittingly picked up or created over time. Just complete the following sentences. Please do *not* think about the answers. Simply write down the *first* thing that comes to mind:

Girls are _____ .

Boys are _____ .

Men are _____ .

Women are _____ .

Teachers are _____ .

Politicians are _____ .

Managers are _____ .

My spouse is _____ .

My neighbor is _____ .

In a college class, the instructor asked us to make a list of all the attributes of a girl and then list the attributes of a woman.

The list for a girl included the words "young, helpless, and pretty." A woman was identified as "independent, professionally dressed and middle-aged." Such descriptions uncover personal beliefs. Even though these beliefs are often unconscious, they affect the quality of your thoughts and the content of what you assume.

If a girl happens to take charge of a situation, you may assume she doesn't understand what's going on and will give bad advice. This is because you believe she is young and helpless. What about your beliefs about men and boys? When a man cries, you might assume he is weak because of a belief that strong men don't show emotion.

Beliefs can be sneaky. You might think you believe one thing and really believe another. You may want to have a different belief than the one you actually accept as true! The first time my husband cried I realized that although I *said* I believe men should be sensitive and show their feelings, I actually had a different belief. His tears made me uncomfortable. *What are you thinking?* I asked myself. I realized I was thinking, *men should be strong!* Yikes! What I wanted to believe was different than what I actually believed.

> **You might think you believe one thing and really believe another.**

Some beliefs about others are outdated. My niece, for example, is graduating from high school this year. When I think about her I see a little girl and assume she is not ready for college. My belief about her creates a story of unpreparedness and immaturity. This story has not been updated to include her tremendous growth during the last few years and it falsely supports negative assumptions about her ability to be on her own.

When you make an assumption about someone or about a situation, one part of that assumption is your belief about the person or situation. Since many beliefs are unconscious, action is required to examine what you are thinking and why. Once you take the action of examination, then you can decide if your beliefs are accurate and helpful or if they need to be adjusted along with your assumptions.

Hey! Don't Think That Way about Yourself!

Beliefs about others are only part of your story. What about the beliefs you have about yourself?

> **For the rest of the day listen to what the voice in your head says *to* you *about* you.**

Try this little mini-project: For the rest of the day listen to what the voice in your head says *to* you *about* you. Did you think, *Great job!* or did you more frequently think *I could have done better*? My friend, Coptic Minister Eric Webster, says that when you look in the mirror, you forget that everything is backwards.

When you view yourself, you are often looking into a backward personal mirror. Negative beliefs are more pronounced than the positive and regular reality checks are necessary to adjust the balance. You tend to remember your "old" self, not incorporating changes you have made and also magnifying areas of weakness. Just like I did with my husband and niece.

My friend did not go to college right after high school because he believed he wasn't "college material." Later, after starting a family, he went to college and was very successful, but it was a stressful experience. Why? After his first good classroom experience, he did not update his personal belief that he was not smart enough for college to incorporate the new information.

> **You tend to remember your "old" self, not incorporating changes you have made and also magnifying areas of weakness. Just like I did with my husband and niece.**

With the outdated belief, he entered every class with negative assumptions and had to fight against those assumptions. It was difficult for him to focus and study and he was constantly worried about failing. Imagine how much more fun and easy class would have been with a new belief saying, "I am very intelligent and learning is something I enjoy."

A woman in a management position is very skilled at finding what motivates people and inspires them to take on new challenges. She believes she is a skilled coach and enjoys this aspect of her job. She also knows she is not exceptionally skilled at interpreting financial reports and often has to ask for help. Unfortunately, she exaggerates her negative belief by saying, "I don't understand finances at all and it's too hard for me." She spends very little time focusing on her positive attributes which keeps her – and others' – focus on the negative.

Do you regularly check in with your beliefs and update them to include new information?

Have any of these scenarios happened to you? Do you regularly check in with your beliefs and update them to include new information? Outdated – and unhelpful – beliefs create inaccurate and often negative stories that form the basis of assumptions.

Ask yourself these questions to determine if your thinking about yourself is helping or holding you back:

- Do I spend more time focusing on and appreciating the positive or negative beliefs about myself?
- Do I consistently add more positive beliefs and remove outdated negative beliefs?
- Do my positive beliefs about myself outnumber the negative ones?

Here's another interesting exercise: Periodically ask yourself, *What am I thinking about myself right now?* Note, mentally or on paper, your thoughts and how they make a you feel. Are they accurate?

As you did when you uncovered your beliefs about others, complete the following sentences to begin to uncover negative or unhelpful beliefs about yourself:

I look _____.

I am the best _____.

I should _____.

I can't _____.

I wish _____.

I'd be happy if _____.

It's not fair that _____.

I am so mad that _____.

Understanding your beliefs about other people and yourself is necessary to stop Crappy Crap thinking. When you don't examine your beliefs, you hand over ownership of how you think, feel, and act to someone else. In the case of The Susan Story, when you don't examine your beliefs, you are likely to blame Susan, the boss, co-workers, and your family for your own feelings as well as anything and everything that subsequently happens. This keeps you captive to forces outside of yourself. When you get to the bottom of "your story, " take responsibility for your beliefs, release Crappy Crap thinking, you unleash *your* power of positive assumptions.

Write, Produce and Direct a New Story

Learning about the stories you make up is a process of asking yourself questions and noticing your thoughts. This analysis leads to uncovering your beliefs which determine the type of script you write.

Each time an assumption is made, you have an opportunity to change the script. The other actors in your story might take a little time to transition to their new roles. The first time I came home with the assumption that my boys and husband did everything they were asked, they didn't know how to react to the changed script!

> **Each time an assumption is made, you have an opportunity to change the script.**

I entered the house assuming they had done their part and if they hadn't, it just meant there was something more important that needed to be done. I was surprised by the tension – and fear, if I'm being honest – that I felt from them when I said "Hi! I am so glad to be home," instead of "Did you get everything done that I asked?" It might take time for others, and you, to get used to new stories, but once you receive the benefits of prosperity, productivity, and peace you will keep writing and others will look forward to the script changes.

Now you know how to change a negative assumption into a positive assumption by separating the facts from the made-up nonsense and then replacing the Crappy Crap thinking with Happy Crap.

What about conflicts? Will you always need to consciously walk through the 3-step process? And, how do you position yourself to make up more Happy Crap and less Crappy Crap?

Once you learn Happy Crap thinking strategies, conflicts won't need to be a source of worry any more. In fact, you will welcome disagreements as they uncover facts for *more* agreement! Your script, even with conflict, will retain a happy ending. Eventually, a positivity habit will make Happy Crap thinking automatic and you won't always have to think about your thinking. We'll talk about positive conflict resolution (yes, it's possible!) and changing a negativity habit. We'll also explore fun tools to help you write more happy stories.

"I'm Mad, but it's Not About You": An Example

My son Erik stomped into the kitchen after school one day, threw open the refrigerator door and barked, "We don't have anything to eat!" and slammed the door shut. My stomach tightened and my fists clenched as I responded from the center of *my* universe.

"I have been working all day and asked you what you needed from the grocery store," I angrily replied. "I do as much as I can around here and it just isn't good enough, is it?" I snapped, my voice rising with each word. Didn't he know I was the leading lady and he was in a supporting role?

Erik turned, leaned against the counter and looked at me. "I *am* mad, Mom, but it's not about *you*."

I was witnessing my son's experience from the center of *my* universe when it was happening from the center of *his* universe. He was the star of the show. I was not even in the picture! My son's comment stung, shocking me into realizing how quickly I took it personally, created negative assumptions, and believed my interpretation to be the "real story." I had written a negative script titled "Unappreciated Mother" and was carrying out the drama.

Even though it felt uncomfortable – okay, it hurt – to have him call me out on my story, I was so glad he did. Now I could write a new script, one with less drama and more "feel good" lines. A story that would bring me closer to my kids. I decided to title my new script "Understanding and Brilliant (and very good looking) Mother!"

CHAPTER SIX

Happy Crap: Conflict Resolution

When my client from the Caribbean Vacation example called back, she told me the "real" story of what had happened to delay her response. When my son snapped at me in the kitchen, he later shared what caused him to feel upset. Is it necessary to know the "truth" about a person or situation for Happy Crap thinking to be effective? Most of the time, whatever is happening is not about you and you don't need to know "why" or "what" or "where," you just need to believe the best and make positive assumptions.

What if You Do Need to Know?

But what if you really do need to know where Susan is going because of your position are at work, relationship to Susan, or for some other reason? What if someone's behavior or comments do need to be addressed? "Are you supposed to make up 'Happy Crap' when you don't have all the information and then just continue on your way and never resolve or confront a conflict?" asked a smart audience member.

> **Happy Crap creates a "positive space holder" to more effectively resolve problems and engage in potentially difficult conversations.**

What if Susan's leaving *is* your concern because you are a supervisor or team leader or even her best friend who is planning a surprise party? Happy Crap thinking is not about avoiding conflict. Happy Crap thinking creates a "positive space holder" to more effectively resolve problems and engage in important conversations. But, before you ask for information, be sure that you really need to know.

Do You Really Need to Know?

Once you have completed the Happy Crap steps in The Susan Story, ask yourself these important questions:

- Do I need to confront Susan about the reason she is leaving work at 4:00 p.m.?
- Is it my business?
- Am I sure?

As you ask yourself these questions, remember that what you perceive is processed from your *personal* perspective; most things are *not* about you. And, even though you might think you clearly see the picture, you probably do not have all the information. If you determine that an issue *does* need to be addressed or more information is required, you can prepare a positive approach to ask for more information to resolve the issue or address any conflict.

3 Truths About Conflict

Truth #1: Conflict is personal. Everything you process goes through your personal filter so that makes everything look – and feel – personal! When someone overlooks you, doesn't pick you for the team, delivers criticism or hurts you in some way (whether it is intentional or not) it feels personal because it is processed from your center.

Truth #2: Conflict is not about you. You process things as personal, but they are rarely about you. In other words, the person(s) or event(s) involved may *include* you, but it is rarely *about* you.

Truth #3: Conflict contains incomplete information. Whether someone is right or wrong or a situation is fair or unfair, the fact remains that you *don't have all the information* because it's impossible to see every angle at once. It is impossible to know exactly what others are thinking and experiencing from their frame of reference. Your personal filter and your perspectives are limited and at least some of the facts are unavailable or obscured.

> **Conflict is personal, not about you, and contains incomplete information.**

If you assume that Susan "snuck" out of the office and intentionally ignored protocol by not getting permission to leave, you work yourself up into a negative state of mind. In this state, you are much less prepared to address any issues. The next day when Susan comes into your office, the hostility you created will be felt by Susan and she, as anyone would, will respond defensively to a perceived attack. Then you respond with more of the same and the conflict escalates instead of becoming resolved. It's important to understand The 3 Truths About Conflict in order to to put the issue in proper perspective for learning and resolution.

Respond Instead of React

So, what do you do when you witness Susan leaving and determine you *do* need to know the full story? Do you run into the parking lot, flag her down, and demand to know where she is going? Reacting (an immediate response) does not allow for Happy Crap thinking and rarely resolves conflict or answers any questions. You need to *respond*, not *react*. But how?

Start by following the three steps to create Happy Crap thinking. Do you remember the steps?

Step 1: Identify the FACTS.

Step 2: Acknowledge your ASSUMPTIONS.

Step 3: Fill in the blanks with HAPPY CRAP.

It is *critical* to immediately substitute Happy Crap thinking for Crappy Crap thinking to create a positive platform from which you can confront a conflict, ask a difficult question, or reveal sensitive feelings. Once you are in a "happy" space, you can more effectively address a potential concern. I use the word, "potential" because you still don't have the whole story, only guesses, about what might have happened or what you think is happening. There might not be any concern or conflict, just fictional Crappy Crap you made up to fill in the blanks!

> **Once you are in a "happy" space, you can more effectively address a potential concern.**

Be Aware of Scarcity Thinking

Scarcity, an inadequate supply, is the predominant social belief and economic model of our country. Scarcity means that the supply of anything is limited, including opportunities and possibilities. If there is a limited supply of everything (goods, services, feelings, opportunities) then it is easy to think that it's just a matter of time before you will not have what you need and want. Scarcity creates fear, worry and suspicion. Each of these instigates and sustains negative thinking.

The opposite of scarcity is abundance. Abundance thinking means you believe there is enough, even more than enough, for everyone. When you believe there are plenty of possibilities, resources, and opportunities for everyone, you feel optimistic and it is natural to choose positive assumptions and easy to hold optimistic thoughts.

When you believe there are plenty of possibilities, resources, and opportunities for everyone, you feel optimistic and it is natural to choose positive assumptions and easy to hold optimistic thoughts.

When you believe that there is enough happiness, love, and wealth to go around, it is logical to believe the best and not be concerned that someone or something is taking your "stuff." When you think the supply of anything is limited, a win/lose mentality takes over and you mentally and physically resist positive assumptions. Positivity works best with "abundance," not "scarcity," thinking.

Hold That Thought

If you need to know where Susan is going or if there truly is some conflict to resolve, make a positive assumption and hold that thought while you follow the five steps to address conflict with a positive approach. As you watch Susan leave, immerse yourself in the most positive reasoning until you believe that whatever is happening will *not* have a negative outcome. Do not proceed until you can hold a Happy Crap assumption.

5 Steps to Happy Crap Conflict Resolution

From a positive position, you are able to identify what needs to be resolved and can address any issues in a way that brings greater clarity and strength to relationships. Five steps are outlined, using The Susan Story, to effectively resolve conflict from a positive perspective. Some steps will happen simultaneously and some will need to be repeated because each resolution is a unique process.

Step 1: Create a Positive Environment. When would it be the best time to talk with Susan? Is it best to call her at home that evening or leave a note on her desk asking to schedule a time to talk? Do you already have a meeting scheduled with her? Pick a time where you will have privacy; both of you will be able to relax. Schedule a meeting as soon as possible. Don't put it off! You are orchestrating a positive environment from which to listen, learn, and create a resolution.

Step 2: Determine Your Motivation. Before addressing the issue with Susan, take a moment to assess your concerns and motivation for confronting Susan. Are you angry that she did not ask your permission, do you feel left out, or is your concern for another reason? There should be a reason other than "because I want to know" to validate your interest.

Step 3: Take Responsibility. Begin the conversation by taking responsibility and sharing your motivation and feelings. Then ask the questions you want answered. Taking responsibility for your beliefs and telling the truth about what you fear, believe, or are concerned about is *critical*. If you own "your stuff," there can be dialogue instead of blame.

Step 4: Listen. After you share your motivation and feelings and ask your questions, put your feelings and ego aside. Expect to hear something reasonable and resolvable, and be open to the response.

> **Expect to hear something reasonable and resolvable, and be open to the response.**

I don't know how many times I have heard "put your feelings aside and listen." It's good advice – or I wouldn't share it with you – but not always easy to do. It is easier after you have taken the first three steps to Happy Crap conflict resolution because you have diffused some of the negativity. However, it can still be a challenge to really hear what someone has to say without being defensive.

What works for me is to visualize putting my thoughts, opinions, and feelings into a bag. Sometimes I visualize a paper lunch bag and other times a gift sack or a tote bag. Whatever I choose, I visualize it in detail. In the bag I put all my feelings and my ego, and gently place the bag in a safe place. Maybe I put the bag by the door so that I can pick it up on my way out. Maybe I tuck it in a closet or leave it in the car. Physically putting aside my own thoughts, opinions, and feelings – even though it's imaginary – allows me to hear someone else without feeling like I am giving up or giving in.

Step 5: Expect the Best. No matter what Susan's response, have a genuine belief that no matter what is said, everything will work out for the best. Resolution is not always immediate so continue Happy Crap thinking for as long as it takes to work through a problem.

You may want to use visualization again and imagine the ideal outcome to the situation or imagine having an amicable lunch with Susan and enjoying each other's company. Hold that thought if resolution doesn't come as quickly as you would like or if the steps do not flow perfectly. The outcome will be whatever you expect it to be even if it takes longer than you would like.

> **Disagreement is an opportunity to better understand each other and ourselves, not a conspiracy to make life harder.**

Creating Happy Crap is not useful if you abandon it at the first sign of struggle. Disagreement is an opportunity to better understand each other and ourselves, not a conspiracy to make life harder. Use the 5 Steps to Happy Crap conflict resolution as many times as you need them.

Must You Agree?

When you positively position yourself in a conflict situation, it does not automatically mean you agree with the other person or feel good about what is happening. You are simply choosing to work from a position of prosperity, productivity and peace that may or may not include agreement.

From a positive position, you can put aside your defenses, tell your truth, and "hear" the other person. Most of the time, even in conflict, all people attempt to act with the best intentions and want to build positive relationships. Your agreement is not necessary to create positive resolution.

> **Your agreement is not necessary to create positive resolution.**

A Conversation with Susan

Steps and instructions sound good, but sometimes when you try them, they feel awkward. Here's a sample conversation with Susan as an example of applying the truths and steps of Happy Crap conflict resolution.

You: "Susan, I felt upset when you left early and did not ask if you could leave. It looked to me like you just took off and left the rest of us to do the work. I am telling you this because it's my job to keep the project on task and because we are friends. I felt left out when you didn't tell me first."

Susan: "I am so sorry! I told the Department Manager I was leaving because my parents had just arrived from out of town and I needed to pick them up from the airport. Martha and I discussed my portion of the project and since I am ahead of the timeline, my leaving early allowed the other areas to catch up. I had planned to call you last night, but I got busy with our guests."

You: "I am so glad you are okay and I'm happy to hear that the project is moving forward. I know you do good work and always meet deadlines. With all the overtime we have been working, and how tired I am, sometimes I miss the progress reports. I do remember you mentioning your parents coming in, but I didn't realize it was this week! Next time something like this occurs, would you please leave me a message or ask Martha to let me know? That way, I can make schedule changes, answer staff questions and cover any work that needs to get done."

Susan: "Of course! Thanks for telling me how you feel and not getting angry. This project has been stressful, but we are such a great team."

Happy Crap Resolution

Positive communication is not only about "happy" talk and thoughts, it's also about difficult conversations and uncomfortable feelings. Positive means "what is for the best." It is rarely "best" to stick your head in the sand and pretend nothing is happening when there is conflict or you feel wrong needs to be righted. It is also rarely "best" to confront conflict from a negative space or by *assuming* the worst. To work through difficult conversations with yourself and others, first create a positive space with Happy Crap. Then tell the truth from *that* space. You will be amazed how much less conflict there is and how much less difficult conversations are.

> **Positive communication is not only about "happy" talk and thoughts, it's also about difficult conversations and uncomfortable feelings.**

Talk with a Teenager: An Example

Remember the story about my son coming home from school angry and announcing that there was nothing to eat? I assumed his anger was about me, and instead of believing the best (such as "he feels like home is a safe place to vent his frustration of the day"), I assumed he was angry with *me*. This story is a good illustration of how quickly a situation can be interpreted negatively and made personal. But, what if his tone of voice and behavior – even though it was not about me – needed to be addressed? In that case, it shouldn't be ignored.

After establishing that Erik had a difficult day, we were able to talk about how to appropriately express angry feelings. Impolite or disrespectful communication should not be ignored or dismissed, even if it's not intended as personal.

> **Impolite or disrespectful communication should not be ignored or dismissed, even if it's not intended as personal.**

"I am so sorry you had a tough day," I said to my son. "Thanks, Mom. I really appreciate you listening and understanding," he shared after telling me the details. "Next time, I would like you to tell me you feel angry instead of snapping at me. I don't feel very good when you talk to me in that angry voice," I shared. "Good point! I wouldn't like it either. I'll try to remember to tell you first how I'm feeling if this happens again," he offered.

First I listened as he told me about his day and created a positive space to address the issue. Then I determined that my motivation to talk with him was not to "be in charge" but to enhance our relationship. Finally, I told my truth and believed that the outcome would be positive. Talking to my son about how I would like to be addressed went so much better after using Happy Crap thinking and conflict resolution.

Allowing my sons – or anyone – talk to me in a way that makes me uncomfortable or feel diminished is not okay. But, attacking back doesn't build good relationships either. Positive conflict resolution strategies allow an issue to be addressed, build relationships, and increase positive feelings. Conflict then becomes an opportunity for increased understanding and more Happy Crap!

CHAPTER SEVEN

Crappy Crap to Happy Crap: The Choice to Change

Gathering with friends, a I used to tell humorous, animated stories about the crap that happened to me during the day or week. A story might begin with "You won't believe how stupid my boss was today!" or "My neighbor always lets his dog walk in our yard, it's no wonder we can't grow grass." I would easily blame others and complain. My friends would laugh and I felt important. But later, when I was alone without the laughter, I sunk into gloom as I kept thinking about those rotten events. I wanted to feel happy and good about my life, but didn't know where to start.

What changed? My thinking became so crappy that my life became crappy too. I hit a Crappy Crap bottom and realized that I had a choice to make. My story wasn't going to have a happy ending if I kept on this way. I couldn't make anyone else change (we've all learned this even though we keep forgetting it) so it had to be me. I made a choice to change my Crappy Crap thinking to Happy Crap.

Misery Loves Company

It can be fun to complain, be dramatic, and tell interesting stories. People bond over shared misery; as the saying goes, "misery loves company!" When a person is negative there is always something to fix, worry about, or fight over which keeps the action and drama high.

Gathering with others to complain and share the latest economic bad news or commiserate about the general crappiness – difficulty– of life can help people feel connected. You are part of the family, team, or group of friends as you are collectively the "run through the wringer." You feel like you fit in and are not alone. If sharing negativity can help you feel united with others, what's so bad about that?

> **Bonding over negativity is destructive as it perpetuates bad feelings and the habit of not taking responsibility for your own happiness.**

There is a difference between telling the truth about difficulties or sharing negative feelings, and *being negative*. Bonding over negativity is destructive as it perpetuates bad feelings and the habit of not taking responsibility for your own happiness. *Sharing difficulties, however, is cathartic and generates positive energy. In this way, you can address issues by taking responsibility for how you are feeling, stating what you believe, and taking any action that needs to be taken.

When you share negativity, you might "fit in" with the crowd, but you also arrest change, growth and prosperity. Do you want to be like everyone else or have a different experience? If you look at any "Who's Who" list, you will find a lot of positive people. Negative people are busy being part of the crowd, whereas positive people are busy living to their fullest potential.

You Know You are Being Negative When:

- You blame others or events for your situation and how you feel.
- You are not open to encouragement or suggestions.
- You are unable to "move past" negative feelings after venting.

Initially, substituting Happy Crap thinking in place of negative assumptions feels uncomfortable. Choosing different thoughts takes effort and your brain wants to return to its comfortable patterns of negative thinking. Choosing Happy Crap thinking doesn't always feel good or easy at first, but it's worthwhile in the end.

Self Evaluation: Are You on The A List?

The first step in making the choice to change your thinking is to evaluate "where you are" right now. A friend of mine read the following two lists and said, "Wow! I know which one I want to be on, but I spend an awful lot of time being on the list I don't want to be on!"

Take a look at both lists and make a check mark next to each statement that describes you.

Items in the first list will probably be easy to check. It's the items in the *second* list that may be a bit more difficult for you to acknowledge. Have the courage to be honest. No one is looking and this exercise provides the insight necessary to choose different thoughts.

	LIST A
	People smile when they think about me
	I remember other people's important life events
	People often remark that I "get them"
	Deep belly laughs are a regular part of my life
	People love to tell me when something wonderful happens to them
	I rarely criticize others
	People trust me to share their biggest fears
	I feel optimistic and hopeful
	People know my flaws and like me anyway
	I am surrounded by people with value systems like mine
	Sunny days are the norm for me no matter what the weather
	People would trust me with their bank book
	I take good care of myself
	I have a specific vision for my future
	TOTAL NUMBER OF CHECK MARKS

	LIST B
	My expectations often go unmet
	The bad things in my life are caused by other people
	In my circle of friends and family, I am often the most unhappy
	My medicine cabinet is unnecessarily full and I see my doctor so often we know each other's birthday
	Food, drugs, sex, cigarettes, and/or alcohol comfort me
	I feel angry a lot
	My job is a huge source of stress for me. I wish I could quit, but I can't
	My family is not close and I rarely spend time with them
	Socializing is more trouble than it's worth
	I feel that I need to point out flaws and mistakes in others
	My "to do" list keeps getting longer and I just can't seem to get things done
	I try to be on time, but I am often late
	Someday I will organize my house and my office
	It seems like it's just one bad thing after another and I never get a break
	TOTAL NUMBER OF CHECK MARKS

Add up the check marks on each list. Does one list have more check marks than the other?

People with the attributes, habits, and attitudes in list "A" generate positive energy toward others and for themselves. Being near people with positive energy feels good. Their optimism, positive assumptions, and overall health make you feel happy and hopeful. "A-listers" have bad times and express sorrow, anger, and frustration; they just don't stay there for any longer than necessary.

> **"A-listers" have bad times and express sorrow, anger, and frustration; they just don't stay there for any longer than necessary.**

People with more attributes, habits and attitudes in list "B" drain others' energy. Have you ever been in someone's presence and then when they left you felt like your energy had been sucked away? Negativity drains energy from everyone, including the negative person themselves. Negative people *do have* good times and express joy, happiness, and hope; they just aren't able to stay there for very long as they tend to assume the worst.

My friend who read the lists and said, "I spend an awful lot of time being the one I don't want to be," is a positive person. She is caring, believes people are good, and takes care of herself and her family. Her comment reminds me that there is room for more optimism in all of us. Understanding your thoughts will help you choose to spend more time on the "A" list no matter who you encounter or what is happening around you.

Stop the Negative Talk

How many negative assumptions and thoughts turn into negative talk? The Greek philosopher, Socrates, said that before relaying a story, you should ask these three questions: Is it true? Is it kind? Is it necessary?

> **The Greek philosopher, Socrates, said that before relaying a story you should ask these three questions: Is it true? Is it kind? Is it necessary?**

Before sharing information, be certain it is true. Then, decide if it shows the people involved in the best light. Would you want this to be said about you? Is it absolutely necessary to pass this on, and are you the best bearer of the information? If the answer to any of these three questions is "no," then you should keep your mouth shut. Pouring your thoughts through Socrates' filters determines if what you are thinking is factual, positive and *needs* to be shared.

Sometimes people forget that just because something is shared with them, they don't have to repeat it. Just because you have a thought, you don't have to say it or hold on to it. Just because someone says something negative to you, doesn't mean you need to respond the same way. The amount of negativity in the world can be reduced by simply filtering your thoughts, recognizing the negative, and making positive replacements.

Start the Positive Talk

Gossip is a mechanism to connect people and you bond with others when you share information. Communicating negative information, however connecting it may be, produces stress and spreads negativity. It makes people, both those listening and those sharing, feel bad.

Consider an alternative. Imagine what it would be like if people only gossiped about others' accomplishments and spread compliments. A person's gifts would be embellished, just as their faults are in negative gossip. Detail would be added to stories of someone helping another, just like specifics are shared in stories of someone disappointing another or not following through on a promise.

Imagine gossiping about a co-worker's accomplishments, "Did you hear about the project that Sally just finished? I think it is the best work she's ever done!" Or imagine talking about a neighbor's good relationship. "My neighbor and his wife eat dinner together by candlelight every night. He reads her poetry and packs her lunch every morning. I am so happy for them."

> **Imagine what it would be like if people only gossiped about others' accomplishments and spread compliments.**

If you only gossiped about others' accomplishments and filled the grapevine with compliments for others you could begin to expect the best. Trust would increase, defenses would drop, and when someone made a mistake, it would easily be forgiven. Hostility might not exist and blame would be obsolete.

Positive gossip boosts your positive brain chemicals, increasing your positivity and productivity. You might be inspired to do more "good" and spread more Happy Crap when you imagine that others will gossip about you in a positive way.

Happiness is just as contagious as negativity. There was a study conducted that showed positivity to spread to three degrees! That means that your happiness spreads to me, which effects my son's mood and is transferred to our neighbor or my son's friend. When you enter a room where negative gossip is happening, you can feel it. Unless you

> **Happiness is just as contagious as negativity.**

leave soon after arriving, you begin to absorb the negativity and may even find yourself adding to it. Stop the spread of negativity by avoiding negative conversations, not repeating unnecessary negative information, and choosing to talk about what is good.

Negativity Is Not Necessary

Isn't some negativity necessary? Without some pessimism – or it least skepticism – wouldn't you lose touch with reality? Many people believe that a certain amount of negativity is necessary to set realistic goals, spot potential problems, and stay grounded in reality. "Imagine the worst-case scenario and then see yourself working through it," is the popular advice for overcoming a fear. This appears to work because you are preparing yourself for the worst. In truth, it's the *second* part of the exercise that makes it effective. Seeing yourself work through the problem and experience *success,* not imagining the worst is what makes this exercise effective. Fear is counteracted by imagining an optimistic outcome, not by any negative fear-based "reality" conjured up in the mind.

Letting go of negativity does change your perspective; you *will* lose touch with *one* reality. You will lose touch with a reality focused on what *doesn't* work, what goes wrong, and negative feelings. This reality includes worrying, blaming, and scarcity thinking.

The danger in letting go of the negativity is not the possibility of becoming a "Pollyanna" (an excessively or blindly optimistic person) and missing critical information, but in staying stuck in negativity. Negativity, not optimism, interferes with your ability to see signs of danger or, for that matter, any opportunities! Some believe that negativity and positivity are two sides to the same coin. Are they? There is no evidence that "good" could not exist without "bad" or vice versa. It is possible that it could be "all good" because, maybe, instead of being two sides to the same coin; they are entirely different currency.

> **Negativity, not optimism, interferes with your ability to see signs of danger or, for that matter, any opportunities!**

If there is any danger in choosing a positive reality, it is experiencing the shock of how much prosperity, productivity, and peace you miss by assuming the worst! When you decide to tell a positive story you open yourself up to opportunities and possibilities no matter what your challenges. You do not lose your ability to spot danger. In fact, you have better radar because it is not jammed with Crappy Crap!

External events, opinions of others, and acts of nature are out of your control. What you *think* about and how you decide to tell the story, remains in your hands. This means you are no longer at the mercy of anything or anyone *outside of yourself.* Without the constraint of negativity, you are free to do anything, help anyone, and be anyone.

Change is in *your* hands. It is *your* choice. Knowing how you benefit and are held back by current thinking habits helps you decide if you need, or want, to change. Ultimately, you must believe that the quality of your thoughts determines the quality of your life. The question then becomes, how do you create a habit of Happy Crap thinking?

Missed Test: An Example

During a semester of teaching, two students – one man and one woman – missed an important exam. They had been warned that make-up exams, except in extraordinary circumstances, would not be granted. The day after the exam, both students came to see me; the difference in the tenor of their visits was remarkable.

The female student, interrupting another class, approached me crying and in a heightened emotional state. She pleaded with me to let her re-take the test. Blaming her absence on her alarm clock having been wedged between her couch cushions, she *insisted* that her future would be ruined if she was not allowed to take the exam. In as understanding a way as I could muster, I expressed my regret for her monumental loss and shepherded her from the room.

The male student, approaching me during my scheduled office hours, asked if he could have a few minutes of my time. He started the conversation by stating that he was not expecting me to offer a make-up test, but only wanted to explain his absence. His girlfriend's car had broken down on the highway and she was very upset. He felt that, although someone else could have helped, he needed to help her. I asked to see some proof of his story and he produced a receipt for car parts. I offered to schedule a make-up exam for him.

The two students experienced the same event: a missed test, but expressed very different reactions. Therefore, they experienced very different outcomes. One assumed the very worst and the other assumed the best. Both students received just what they thought they would.

Choosing to assume the best takes courage and trust that all will work out as it should. The male student knew that even if he received a zero on the test, his life would neither be ruined nor his opportunities disappear. The female student, on the other hand, chose not to take responsibility for her thinking and—in effect—masterminded her own tragedy.

CHAPTER EIGHT

A Happy Crap Habit

A habit is a behavior you repeat over and over until it becomes automatic. Habits themselves are neither good nor bad. It is the *outcome* of the habit that determines whether a pattern should be maintained or changed. When deciding if you want to change your thinking, the question to ask yourself is " do the assumptions I make up help and serve me, or do they hurt and control me?"

You probably brush your teeth every day and it has become a habit. Does the outcome help or hurt you? Clean teeth and fresh breath help your overall health and possibly your personal relationships, so you want to keep this habit. What do you routinely do that doesn't help you? Consider your thinking habits. Do you have more positive or negative thoughts? Do your thinking habits help you gain prosperity, productivity, and peace?

The Deer Path

Habits are created when repeated behaviors, including mental behaviors such as negative thinking form neural pathways in specific regions of the brain. Imagine the paths deer make through tall grass. Deer take the same trails time after time until the grass becomes flat. Maybe the paths lead to food, water, or shelter sources. After the deer create the trails, they no longer need to think about where to go when they are hungry, thirsty, or tired; they just walk and end up at the place that satisfies their basic needs. That's what happens with habits. Your brain automatically travels the paths most worn.

One day, however, the deer travel down a path and do *not* find food, water, or shelter. Something has changed. Each time the deer feel the stimulus, whether it's hunger, thirst, or fatigue, they travel a well-worn path. Since the source – or reward – for traveling a path has dried up, the deer is unsatisfied. But, the deer continue to make trips down the path several times before realizing a change is needed.

Every habit you have began as a behavior – physical or mental – that helped you. You repeated the action enough for it to become habit. Once a habit is established, even if it is no longer necessary or has stopped being helpful, it takes effort to create new neural pathways for new patterns. Each time an old way is resisted and a new way chosen, the grass grows to cover the old pathway and the grass is compressed to create the new pathway.

Damage Assessment: Motivation to Change

Lori and Gregory Boothroyd, authors of *Going Home – A Positive Emotional Guide for Promoting Life-Generating Behaviors* teach that most self-defeating behaviors (unhelpful habits), such as making negative assumptions, are formed in childhood and originally served a purpose to protect us. As children, negative assumptions may have helped us avoid a playground bully. As adults, such negativity holds us back from forming significant relationships. Understanding the full impact of a self-defeating behavior can provide the motivation to create new mental habits – deer paths – that help. The new habits replace habits that no longer give you what you need.

> As children, negative assumptions may have helped us avoid a playground bully. As adults, such negativity holds us back from forming significant relationships.

In Step 4 of the Boothroyds' 12-step process a damage assessment tool is explained (for information about the full process visit www.loriboothroyd.com). By using this tool you are able to identify outcomes – or results – of a self-defeating behavior. The physical, mental, emotional, relational, and financial effects of a negative behavior become obvious and this knowledge can be used as motivational fuel for change. When I first assessed the impact of negative assumptions for me, I was surprised to find so many areas of my life affected.

To conduct your own damage assessment, draw a small circle in the middle of a piece of paper. Write "negative assumptions" in the center of this circle and ask yourself what happens as a result of making negative assumptions. Draw circles branching out from the main circle. In each circle write the things that happen or feelings you have as a result of choosing negative assumptions. From each of those circles, branch off more circles to uncover more outcomes.

When you realize the harm from making negative assumptions you can decide if you want or need to change your current thinking habits. Here is part of my damage assessment. Some circles are blank so you can practice by adding to mine before making your own damage assessment.

Negative Assumptions Damage Assessment

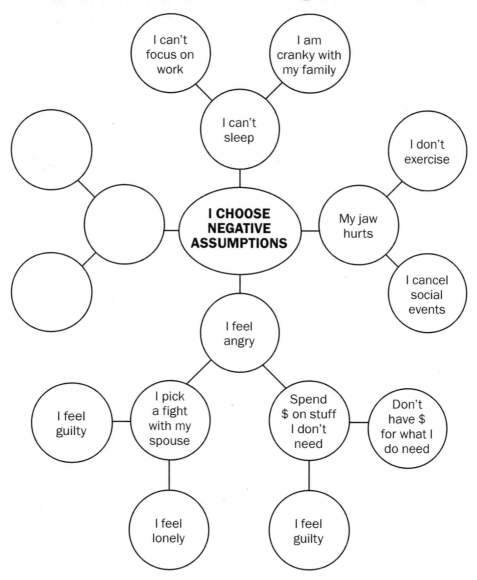

Damage Assessment: The Susan Story

Let's use The Susan Story as a case study for a damage assessment and examine the specific physical, emotional, and financial consequences of making negative assumptions about Susan, both in the short and long terms.

Physically, your body tensed up when you made negative assumptions about Susan's leaving. Studies show that anger, worry, and fear cause a "fight or flight" response. These physiological responses pull blood away from vital organs, weaken memory, and flood the body with stress hormones.

Your body quickly returns to normal if you let the anger go, but carrying the negativity with you continues the cascade of stress hormones, wearing down your organs and immune system. In the short term, an influx of stress hormones may cause a headache, impaired concentration, or possibly some unhealthy snacking. Long-term activation of the stress response increases susceptibility to all kinds of physical ailments, such as colds, accidental injury, and even cancer. Chronic negativity entrenches the deer paths of unhealthy habits that also improve your chances of disease and depression.

Emotionally, you felt upset when you had negative feelings about Susan leaving. Even one negative encounter has emotional effects. How productive are you when you are angry, worried or stressed? After assuming the worst about Susan, perhaps you became short-tempered with your children, or argued with your spouse over something trivial such as folding the laundry. Focusing on

> **Even one negative encounter has emotional effects. How productive are you when you are angry, worried or stressed?**

work, family, and self-care becomes difficult when your mind is negatively engaged with thoughts of where Susan went. If you carry this Crappy Crap thinking into the future, you will create negative beliefs that affect the quality of your assumptions about other people and future events.

How could making negative assumptions have a *financial effect*? Your frustration with the day might have resulted in a decision to go out for dinner rather than cook the meal you'd planned. Or perhaps you spent time on-line or at the mall indulging in a little "retail therapy." Eventually, accumulated stress may lead to spending personal savings on visits to the doctor rather than a vacation.

Mistakes made at work could delay, or derail, a laser-focused career path. Creating negative assumptions might block personal opportunities because others sense your negativity. Your negativity creates a barrier to seeing available options.

> **Creating negative assumptions might block personal opportunities because others sense your negativity.**

To be sure, having *one* negative thought is not going to physically, emotionally, or financially destroy you. Consistent negative thinking, however, will take its toll and limit success, decrease happiness, and impair your health.

Stop Negative Assumptions

If you decide that making negative assumptions is more harmful than helpful, you can change this habit. Like any other habit, however, stopping negative assumptions can be a challenge. How challenging? In his book *Goal Free Living: How to Have the Life You Want Now!*, author Stephen Shapiro says that of the 45 percent of Americans who make resolutions on the last day of the year, only 8 percent *always* achieve success. He goes on to share that three out of four people who set a goal for the New Year almost never follow through.

Does this mean you shouldn't try? Not at all! Changing your Crappy Crap thinking habit may be tough, but you *can* be successful on the first try. If the first try doesn't work, you can keep trying until your changes stick. After all, it's the *follow-through* that most people struggle with. Deciding right now to continue trying, even if there's a lot of starting and stopping, will make a world of difference in your success.

There is no rule that you have to wait until December 31st to resolve to change, or that you must wait for a new year to try again if you stumble. The good news about changing your thought habits is that you have unlimited opportunities to try again every day, every hour, even every minute!

> **Deciding right now to continue trying, even if there's a lot of starting and stopping, will make a world of difference in your success.**

Create a Happy Crap Habit

There are five steps – and one secret ingredient – to successfully making or breaking a habit: motivation, benefits, trigger events, substitute behavior, and a plan. Breaking a habit doesn't happen by closing your eyes tight and wishing really hard. Habits are broken by repetitive effort in a new direction. Together, these habit-kicking components form a recipe to create a Happy Crap habit so that you can have your cake and eat it too!

> **There are five steps — and one secret ingredient — to successfully making or breaking a habit: motivation, benefits, trigger events, substitute behavior, and a plan.**

Let's talk about each step and then work through a plan. You will answer four questions. Your answers to these questions will provide the information to create your personal plan for change. You will build your own recipe for a Happy Crap habit and I have shared mine so you can see what works for me.

Add yourself to the mix:

Why Should I Care? First, understand your motivation to make a new habit. Why are you changing the quality of your assumptions? In order to be successful you need to know why you are putting forth the effort to change and your reason(s) must be for you, not to please someone else. People are most successful in making a significant change when the motivation is specific and pertinent to them. If the motivation is to please someone else or to achieve a social standard, it won't withstand the challenges that accompany changing a habit.

Stir in some personal benefits:

What's In It For Me? Know the specific benefits to you from making a change. With a new habit, what specifically will change for you? Knowing exactly how you will benefit directly and indirectly will keep you focused. How will your health, relationships, and overall lifestyle improve? Saying, "things will be better" or "I will be happier" is not specific enough. Exactly what will change? What will your life look like? Give yourself detailed examples.

Understand your cooking mechanism:

What Sets Me Off? Identify your trigger moments. Which situations spark the behavior you are trying to change? It may be a person, place, time of day, or a physical condition such as stress, fatigue, or hunger that triggers the automatic habit response. If you know your triggers, you can create a strategy to stop the automatic reaction and interrupt with a replacement thought.

Drain the Crappy Crap:

What Replaces Negative Assumptions? Replace a self-defeating behavior with a life-affirming behavior. Determine which behaviors and thoughts you will substitute for the old behavior. When the opportunity arises to make a new choice, know in advance what action you will substitute. When a trigger moment is identified, there are only a few seconds to replace an old strategy with a new behavior. Knowing exactly what to substitute and planning how you'll do it is essential to change the course of a habit.

Add the secret ingredient:

I Am A Warrior! Finally, no matter what, don't stop! Try and try again! How long will it take? Habit changes take multiple *intentional* actions. Don't stop until it becomes automatic. Some professionals say that changing a habit takes twenty-one consecutive days, but it depends on the habit. The deeper the emotion involved, the longer it takes. Don't be discouraged if it takes longer than you think it should. Habits involving people can take *years* to reprogram. Think about the time it took to develop a habit and acknowledge that it could take more than a month to make lasting changes.

Stir and enjoy!

Now you have the recipe for a Happy Crap habit! You can create a perpetual sweet life whenever and for as long as you want. Complete the recipe by adding your plan to the mix and you will end up with a Happy Crap habit with unlimited access to prosperity, productivity and peace.

Let's make a plan to stop negative assumptions using the five ingredients. Answer the questions by finishing the following sentences to build your own Happy Crap plan. You *are* going to make up crap, so personalize each step to create a habit of assuming Happy Crap. After you build your plan, you can take a look at how I designed my Happy Crap plan.

Your Happy Crap Plan

To create your personalized Happy Crap Plan, write out the following questions on a piece of paper and answer each one in detail. Leave room to add more and make changes as you put your plan into action.

Why Should I Care? I am motivated to choose positive assumptions when I don't have all the facts because:

What's In It For Me? The specific benefits for me of choosing positive assumptions are:

What Sets Me Off? The events, people and circumstances that trigger negative assumptions for me are:

What Replaces Negative Assumptions? Positive behaviors I could substitute in place of negative assumptions are:

I Am A Warrior! Ways I will support myself to continue changing my behavior until a new habit is formed are:

The Positive Results Are Worth It

I have stopped and started many habits. I've added regular exercise to my life, developed healthy eating habits, quit smoking, stopped drinking alcohol, changed my thinking, and begun making financial choices to move toward fiscal independence. For each, I have gone through the five steps to successfully making or breaking a habit. All of the habits have taken more time to stop or established than I expected.

My mental deer paths were well-worn and negative thinking was an automatic part of my life. It took time to distinguish assumptions from facts because I thought many of my assumptions *were* facts. Working on my beliefs, I realized I do choose my thinking and I had chosen a lot of Crappy Crap! Once I realized the damage that came from making negative assumptions, I decided to take action to replace my Crappy Crap thinking with Happy Crap.

Choosing positive instead of negative assumptions has been the most challenging of my habit changes. It's also been the most rewarding. Choosing new thinking patterns has made other changes easier and has had a positive impact on all areas of my life.

Erika's Happy Crap Plan: An Example

Why Should I Care? I am motivated to choose positive assumptions when I don't have all the facts because:

- *I want to feel happy more often and to have long-term, close relationships in all areas of my life.*

What's In It For Me? The specific benefits for me of choosing positive assumptions are:

- *Feeling more at peace because I am less anxious at the end of the day and that helps me choose not to snack in front of the television.*
- *Not nit-picking at my kids because I focus on the good they have done, instead of what they have not done. More harmony in my house.*
- *Believing the best about my work and that my clients will help me be more creative. My ideas and dreams will become a reality with positive thinking.*

What Sets Me Off? The people, events, and circumstances that trigger negative assumptions for me are:

- *Having unrealistic expectations of myself makes me see the worst instead of the best. Too much on my "to-do" list gets me every time.*
- *When my husband or sons are in a bad mood, I "catch" their mood.*
- *Lacking enough sleep or being too hungry triggers many negative assumptions.*

What Replaces Negative Assumptions? Positive behaviors I will substitute in place of negative assumptions:

- *When someone does not answer me right away (in person, phone or e-mail), I immediately imagine a best-case scenario.*
- *When one of my husband or sons has a bad day or is in a "mood," I tell them I love them and remove myself from the situation until they have time to feel a bit better.*
- *Eat regular, healthy meals throughout the day so I am never too hungry.*
- *Set a bedtime and stick to it as often as possible to get enough sleep.*

I Am A Warrior! Ways I will support myself to continue changing my behavior until a new habit is formed are:

- *Congratulate myself for recognizing a negative assumption and create a positive assumption I could use the next time I am in the same situation.*
- *Make any necessary apologies to others, including one to myself.*
- *If I realize I am taking action based on negative assumptions, I will immediately look for opportunities to consciously make positive assumptions. I will then choose new actions based on my changed thinking.*

CHAPTER NINE

Happy Crap Toolbox:
8 Positive Assumption Strategies

When you choose to make up Happy Crap to fill in the blanks, good things will happen. Not only will you feel immediately better (Happy Crap cannot co-exist with fear, blame, or worry), but your relationships will be enhanced. Tension will mysteriously disappear and you will be better able to hear and calmly respond to people in your life. Most importantly, your relationship with yourself will change as you treat yourself to happy thoughts and stop creating positivity roadblocks. Happy Crap thinking is the epitome of self-care!

It's fun to make up Happy Crap the first few times because it is novel and exciting, like a new job, new relationship, or new hobby. After a while, however, the excitement can fade. Faced with some life challenges, it can be easy to "forget" that you choose your thoughts and get right back to your Crappy Crap thinking habit.

The other day a friend and I were talking about choosing healthy foods and how in some situations it's easier to make good choices than it is in others. We discussed the different tools and strategies we use and what works and what doesn't. She said, "Different tools work on different days; sometimes several tools are needed and sometimes nothing seems to work!" What's important is that you have some tools available to help you choose Happy Crap. I've filled a toolbox just for you!

Here are eight positive assumption strategies (tools). We'll discuss each tool, to help you develop and maintain a Happy Crap thinking habit:

1. Check your body

2. Eliminate Crappy Crap words

3. Share "Three Good Things"

4. Sit on the floor

5. Catch it in a glove

6. Create space for Happy Crap

7. Energize yourself with play

8. Declare today the very best day ever!

While new brain pathways are being created to make Happy Crap thinking a habit, these tools will help you choose positive assumptions, especially during challenging situations. Use the tools alone or in any combination and add more as you discover your own!

Tool #1: Check Your Body

This tool could be called the "Master" tool because it fits any situation, and sometimes is enough by itself. Before you can substitute Happy Crap thinking for Crappy Crap thinking, you will need to recognize your pessimistic response. Each person has physical cues occurring directly before and during negative thoughts.

How does your body respond just before, during, or after a Crappy Crap thought? Right now, imagine something you are worried about, and assume the worst. How do you feel? What is your body's reaction?

Physical reactions vary depending on the person and situation. The following physical responses are all possible signs that negative assumptions are being made:

- Hunched shoulders
- Head pain or throbbing temples
- Hands clenched into fists
- Leaning away from someone (when seated or standing)
- Narrowed eyes
- Tight jaw
- Inability to make eye contact

List five physical responses you have as you imagine yourself in a negative situation making up Crappy Crap.

Choose one of your physical responses and be aware of it over the next week. Whenever you have this physical reaction, substitute Happy Crap thinking for any negative assumptions threatening to pop up. Knowing your body's reactions to negativity provides an opportunity to substitute positive assumptions and create a Happy Crap habit.

Tool #2: Eliminate Crappy Crap Words

HAVE to I'll TRY
Stressed!
Can't Mad!
Busy You NEVER
It's not FAIR
Shouldn't
I NEVER Tired
Must
I wish

Word choices often enable and perpetuate negativity. There's the "b" word, the "s" word and the dreaded "f" word. "Busy," "Stressed" and "not Fair" are commonly used Crappy Crap words. People often—and easily—use negative words and are usually unaware that just saying these words creates *more* Crappy Crap thoughts.

My sons know that I would rather they use swear words than Crappy Crap words. Swear words are negative, but they are obviously negative. Crappy Crap words are deceptive. There's a hidden danger because they are so readily used and accepted. What seemingly harmless negative words do you use every day? Think about how often you say, "should", "have to", "can't", and even "I wish"? Take a look at the words above. Do you use any of them? Listen to yourself for one day and hear how often Crappy Crap words are spoken.

Then, play a word game, "Pessimism" Scrabble®, to get a powerful perspective on the impact of using negative words. See if you can come up with one sentence using as many Crappy Crap words as possible. If you think of a negative word or phrase that is not listed, feel free to add it.

Have you heard or said any variation of the following sentences?

"I wish I could have lunch with you today, but I can't because I am so stressed and busy and have to get my work finished."

"I know I shouldn't go out to dinner again this week, but I can't find time to get to the store because I am so busy and you never schedule appointments with enough notice!"

"I am so mad that Susan gets to leave early because it's just not fair that I have to stay here and all I ever get is more work and no appreciation!"

Listen carefully to the conversations of people around you. Then listen to yourself. Are you using language to create more negativity in your life? Crappy Crap thoughts are expressed with negative words. Using a vocabulary filled with negative verbiage, you're more prone to accepting Crappy Crap thinking because that's how you're used to speaking. When you "outlaw" the Crappy Crap words, you'll find a more positive way of looking at things and expressing yourself.

> **With a vocabulary filled with negative verbiage, you're more prone to accepting Crappy Crap thinking because that's how you're used to speaking.**

Begin by removing one negative word from your vocabulary and notice how your thoughts, feelings, and conversations are affected. Many years ago, an acquaintance I had hoped would become a friend, commented on my use of Crappy Crap words. "You say 'mad' and 'angry' a lot," she shared. "I don't know if I want to be around someone as angry as you."

Embarrassed and shocked by her observation, I spent the next couple of days listening to my self-talk and conversations. Her comment was confirmed by my own observations. I used "angry" talk a lot, which expressed my core feelings. Using negative words reinforced my negative feelings. I continue to work diligently to keep the "angry" words from my speech and regularly audit myself for other Crappy Crap words. If I notice too many negative words, I review my Happy Crap plan and decide where and how to make changes.

Tool #3: Share "Three Good Things"

In my first book, *Three Good Things: Happiness Every Day, No Matter What!* I shared the story of how my husband and I over-came our negativity by focusing on the "good," instead of the "bad" moments at the end of each day.

Early in our marriage, my husband and I were miserable. We weren't getting what we wanted: new jobs, fun adventures, weight loss, or a happy relationship. We complained, whined and felt sorry for ourselves to the point where we blamed each other for our unhappiness. I worried that maybe we weren't right for each other.

At the height of our negativity, I met some people at work who were so happy and seemed to always expect the best. It struck me that they were not wealthier, better educated, or more successfully employed than me. They were, however, better off in their enjoyment of life.

One day on my way home from work, I was determined to find a way to happiness. Arriving at home, I announced to my husband that neither of us could say anything negative until we had shared at least three good things.

That first day was grueling. My husband insisted *nothing* positive happened during the day. I *insisted* we come up with at least three good things.

"Was your coffee hot?" I asked.

"No!" he responded.

"Did someone tell a joke or find a quarter?" I asked.

"I know!" he said. "I saw a deer on my way to work."

"Great! Now, just two more things." I insisted.

It took us a long time to complete our lists. At least it seemed like a long time! But each day it became easier and each evening we spent less time complaining after sharing our "good" lists with each other.

Sharing good things about *your* day, every day, no matter what the events of the day, brings your attention to what is *working*. Spending just five minutes each day sharing at least three good things with your family, co-workers, or friends quickly develops your Happy

> **Sharing good things about *your* day, every day, no matter what the events of the day, brings your attention to what is *working*.**

Crap habit. The more "good" you identify, the more "good" you will assume.

In 2007, Borgess Medical Center in Kalamazoo, Michigan conducted a research study to determine the impact of a gratitude practice using *Three Good Things: Happiness Everyday, No Matter What!* on the happiness of bedside nurses. The results were so positive that the researchers are replicating the study at other hospitals and conducting a new study using *Three Good Things* with teams! In addition to this formal study, many of my clients have enjoyed amazing results by incorporating *Three Good Things* into meetings, staff development processes, and customer service initiatives.

Tool #4: Sit on the Floor

Negative thinking is a psychological perspective that can be altered by simply shifting physical perspective. Changing physical space jars your brain from the usual thinking patterns, forcing it to shift from automatic to manual operation. In automatic, you make the same decisions you always make. In manual, you have choices.

Think back to the last multi-session class you attended. Did you sit in the same seat each class? Do you drive the same way to work each day? At the grocery store, do you follow the same pattern each time you shop? Your physical routines reinforce your mental patterns. *Changing location physically changes you mentally.*

I invite you to try this exercise: From where you are sitting right now, for three minutes, make a list of everything you see. If you run out of things to write before your three minutes are up, look harder and keep writing. Now change your location; move to another part of the room and face a different direction. If you can, sit on the floor. For the next three minutes, from this new location, make another list of everything you see.

Compare your lists. Are they the same? You probably noticed some things from the second location that were not visible from your initial position. If you had all day, how many different positions could you take? Wherever you are physically or mentally offers only *one* option. There are so many options and possibilities right before you. They are, however, impossible to see from your current position.

When you find yourself stuck in negative thinking, try changing your physical location. One of my clients, Kelly, goes for a walk or finds a new place in her building to do her work when office politics degrades the quality of her thinking. In fact, today, I am writing this from a library instead of my office. I allowed myself to get sucked into worry-thinking and I decided to use the "Sit on the Floor" tool to loosen my worry so I could talk with you.

> **When you find yourself stuck In negative thinking, try changing your physical location.**

There are other ways you can change your physical space. For example, changing routines and creating new ways for your body to move. When you find you've slipped into Crappy Crap thinking, altering your physical space is one of the easiest and most effective things to do. Try these ideas for a new physical position:

- Travel a different route to a familiar place such as work, picking up children, or visiting a friend.
- Start at the "opposite" end of the grocery store.
- Eat lunch for breakfast and breakfast for lunch.
- Brush your teeth with your non-dominant hand.
- Try a new sport, exercise class, or different time of day to work out.
- Run a meeting backwards (going from the bottom of your agenda to the top), change the meeting location, or sit in different seats.
- If you are in conflict with someone, try both moving the conversation to another room *and* sitting on the floor.

Tool #5: Catch It in a Glove

If you are anything like me, it is very difficult not to take things personally. The truth is, everything *is* personal because it is filtered through *your own* perspective. What other people say or do often *appears* to be about you, but rarely is. When you hear or see something that is different from what you believe or expect, you "take it personally" and Crappy Crap thoughts are created before you realize what's happening.

How do you stop Crappy Crap thinking when someone says or does something you don't like? Catch it in a glove! A former student taught me this tool and no sports experience is necessary.

"When someone says something to me that I don't like, I catch it in an imaginary baseball glove," my student explained. She visualized having a glove on her right hand and when someone offered her negative advice, criticism, or opinions, she imagined the words going into the glove. She would carry the information around in her imaginary baseball glove for awhile before deciding what she wanted to do – if anything – about it.

Not too long after learning this technique, a friend forcefully criticized me for backseat-driving. I put on my imaginary baseball glove and caught the information. Carrying it around for a couple of days, I watched my behavior. She was right; I was an irritating passenger. I threw away my friend's unkind comments and kept the helpful information. Catching it in a glove allowed me to gain valuable information and avoid Crappy Crap thinking.

Tool #6: Create Space for Happy Crap

In many conversations, especially difficult ones, a pause is needed to determine if you are creating a negative assumption. You need time to put on your Happy Crap thinking cap to keep incoming information neutral and create positive assumptions.

When someone shares something that causes any of the physical responses you discovered in Tool #1, try saying any of the following phrases to give yourself time to choose positive assumptions:

- "Thank you for sharing!"
- "That's good to know."
- "That must be hard for you."

These statements do two things: 1) they give you space to put on a glove or position yourself to distinguish facts from crap, and 2) they help you acknowledge the person who is speaking and provide them with a pause so they can choose to move past their own negative assumptions.

As you use these statements, you will develop space-making statements of your own. When someone says, "I don't agree!" in response to my beliefs, ideas, or opinions, I reply, "Good, now we have an opportunity to understand each other better."

I created that sentence to make space for myself, but also to give the other person space to release any Crappy Crap thinking. When everyone feels safe, it is easier to put down defenses and work toward understanding.

Tool #7: Energize Yourself with Play

Negativity flourishes in tired, hungry and stressed bodies. Unfortunately, in our society this compromised state of being is seen as "normal." When your body and mind are taxed, your "fight or flight" response is triggered. This means that when someone approaches you, even with an innocent comment or request, it can feel like an attack. When you realize you've snapped at someone for no reason, you apologize and say something like, "I'm sorry, I'm just so tired!"

It takes conscious thoughtfulness to distinguish between assumptions and facts. It takes energy to stop Crappy Crap thinking and choose Happy Crap assumptions until new patterns begin to emerge and new habits are formed. Energy is also required to maintain Happy Crap thinking.

> **Play is a great way to create energy. But, people often feel that play is not important, they don't know how to play, or they don't have time.**

There are many ways to energize yourself. You know most of them. It's the "doing" that can be a challenge. Play is a great way to create energy. But, people often feel that play is not important, they don't know how to play, or they don't have time. But, play is essential to renew your energy. If you have children, you may have more opportunity to do playful things. However, the play I'm referring to is simply engaging in activities that delight your body and mind. These may be the same or different from those that delight children. Engaging in your own play releases and nourishes positivity.

When my children were young, I wished for just one day or even a few hours to myself to do anything I wanted, often daydreaming about all that I would do. But the first time an opportunity presented itself, I was unprepared. My husband and sons left the house for an afternoon and I had unexpected free time. But, I had no idea what I wanted to do! By the time I figured it out, they had returned. Has this ever happened to you?

To make sure it did not happen again, I made a list of ways to play in preparation for the next spontaneous occurrence of free time. I have since realized that play is more than something for amusement or rest; it is essential to choosing Happy Crap thinking. Things that are essential to your health should not be left to chance. Schedule play dates with yourself (no children required) to add positive energy and more Happy Crap to your life.

You can make your own "play" list and keep a copy at home, at work and in the car. Then schedule time (even just a few minutes) each day, or at least once a week, for play. My list is on the next page. Feel free to adopt my list or adapt it as a starting point for yours.

Erika's Ways to Play

- Color
- Draw & Paint
- Swing
- Play music on a musical instrument or use a rock and sticks
- Listen to music
- Sing ... loud and everywhere
- Dance
- Exercise for fun
- Skip (I met a Skip and he offered to skip with me!)
- Call my friends & say, "Can you come out & play?"
- Play dress-up (using my closet, a friend's closet, or at the store)
- Pretend
- Cook
- Blow bubbles in my office or in the car
- Pick or buy flowers
- Visit a farm
- Pick apples
- ... Share Three Good Things!

Tool #8: Declare Today the Very Best Day Ever!"

When someone asks, "How are you?", what do you say? You might reply "fine," "good", or "okay." These responses all open the door for Crappy Crap thinking. The next time you use any of these responses, or hear someone else use them, listen to the amount of positive energy in these words. Do you hear any? I suspect not much or any at all.

Perhaps the most powerful Happy Crap tool is to actively assume today is the the very best day ever, every day. When asked, "How are you?" quickly and energetically respond, "Today is my very best day ever!"

"But what if it's not?" you ask.

It is! Yesterday is a memory and *tomorrow* a hope. Today is the only day that exists so it *has* to be your very best day.

"How are you?" is asked so many times a day that it is a grand opportunity to make your Happy Crap commitment. When you say, "Today is my very best day ever!" you declare Happy Crap no matter what the external circumstances. Each time you make this declaration, your Happy Crap habit is being formed and strengthened.

"Today is my very best day ever!" has a bonus side effect. It helps others feel good. If you call a friend of mine at her office, her voice mail will tell you, "I hope you are having your very best day ever!" She tells me that it made her feel great to add this declaration and she gets many positive responses from others who hear it. Declare your very best day, today and every day!

CHAPTER TEN

Live a Happy Crap Life

A Happy Crap life is not one moment of realization and a single choice to think happy thoughts, but a continuous practice of choosing positive assumptions. Any life, happy or not, has its ups and downs. A Happy Crap life has noticeably more ups than downs. Writers of Happy Crap scripts choose their life story so they can enjoy the good, learn from their challenges, and feel happy every day, no matter what their circumstances!

Unleash Your Power

Assumptions are powerful and they are in your control. That is what makes assumptions *your* power. You have absolute domain over your thoughts. It is very important to exercise your power. This is how you unleash your ability to determine how you think, what possibilities and choices you see for yourself, and how you feel.

Each assumption you make becomes your internal dialogue, daily marching order, and life story-line. If you choose your assumptions, it won't matter what life circumstances you are dealt because you will retain control.

> **Each assumption you make becomes your internal dialogue, daily marching order, and life story-line.**

People facing the same occurrences can experience life very differently depending on the quality of their thoughts. In the 1989 movie, *Parenthood*, starring Steve Martin, he plays an uptight, worried father, co-parenting with a go-with-the-flow optimist mother. At the end of the movie, one of their children brings down the school play, literally, by destroying the set. Martin tenses up with embarrassment while his wife laughs and enjoys the new production.

When Martin's character sees his wife laughing he remembers that she referred to life as "a fun roller coaster ride." When he changes his assumptions about the situation, he transforms his fear, worry, and stress into happiness and joy.

There are so many options in front of you that are not visible because negative thinking keeps them out of your line of sight. Paths, options, and resources that were invisible will be revealed when you choose positive assumptions. Martin's character in *Parenthood* was shown an option for an enjoyable experience – a positive adventure – when he chose to make up Happy Crap.

A Promise to Yourself

Promise yourself *right now* that you will use your power.

A Happy Crap life begins when you make a promise to yourself to craft positive assumptions every time you can. This promise, however, is not a command, criticism, or another thing you "should" do. It is a loving pledge

> **Promise yourself *right now* that you will use your power.**

from yourself to treat yourself with kindness. This means you will make positive assumptions about yourself as well as people and things outside of you.

When you find yourself feeling angry, worried, or sad and thinking negative thoughts, do not add to the negative with a verbal reprimand. Instead add a dash of Happy Crap. Congratulate yourself for taking this journey. Compliment yourself on your positive qualities and thank yourself for being yourself today. What would you say to your best friend? That's who you are and what you want to say to yourself.

As part of your promise to yourself, make a promise to be patient with yourself. It takes time to change a well-worn path – habit – of thinking. When Crappy Crap thinking occurs, be kind to yourself, use Happy Crap tools, and gently choose to make positive assumptions. You will feel and see benefits the first time and every time you choose to substitute Happy Crap thinking for Crappy Crap thinking and before long, you won't be changing but maintaining a Happy Crap habit.

When I do talks, I ask people to raise their right hand and take a happiness pledge. They repeat after me as we make the promise together to choose positive assumptions. Feel free to use this pledge. You can print it from my website at www.erikaoliver.com or make your own.

Happy Crap Pledge

I am taking the Happy Crap Pledge that includes sharing Three Good Things each day as a part of my commitment to making positive assumptions.

• • •

"I am ready to be happy."

• • •

"I promise to choose a positive perspective."

• • •

"I will share Three Good Things about my day and make up Happy Crap every day…no matter what!"

Signed:_____ Date:___/___/___

Script Development

Write a new script, literally, for your life. I use two versions of personal script development; one involves writing and the other is about drawing.

Imagine a time in the future, as far ahead as you would like to go (I recommend five years for the first script draft). The script I work from is twenty years out and was developed after writing several five year stories. Visualize a day in that future time and describe it as if you were there right now. Use present tense, include all the people you want there (they do not have to be in your current life) and be specific by describing the day in detail. A sentence from my script reads, "I am sitting in our first cabin and listening to my sons (now grown with their own families) and my husband tease each other as they put away the fishing boat. Even though we now live in our dream house in North Carolina we kept this spot because it means so much to us." Now it's your turn to write a detailed account of your vision.

Another script development technique is to pick a time in the future, as with the first exercise, and draw your perfect day using only pictures and no words. Use crayons or other fun art tools. Just draw and don't write any descriptions. When you don't censor yourself, ideas and beliefs will emerge that are true for you. You may discover, as I did, that you have some dreams you didn't know about! The picture I use as my guide shows me and my husband holding hands walking briskly down an ocean beach. This picture is the reason I started and continue my health and wellness routine. I realized I would need to be healthy and happy for this scene to materialize.

Both script development exercises have been immensely helpful to me in my recovery from pessimism. With a positive script for the future, you can use your power to craft assumptions and write a daily dialogue for your life.

Putting It into Practice

Some days I really struggle to make up Happy Crap. Developing a Happy Crap habit is not something that happens all at once. It is a process. Recently I drove an hour and a half to see a friend who was visiting from

> **Developing a Happy Crap habit is not something that happens all at once. It is a process.**

another state. While driving home I felt tension in my shoulders and realized that my breathing was shallow. What was I thinking? I was thinking about the list of chores I had left for my sons. I imagined them watching television instead of completing their tasks. I was thinking about the work I didn't finish and my upcoming deadlines. I was envisioning disappointed clients. I was thinking about a telephone call I had not made.

Where did this thinking come from? I had just had a good visit with my friend and had no reason for my negativity. I made a list of the facts regarding my thoughts and realized that there was no evidence for my negative thinking. I didn't know what my sons were doing. My work for the next day was finished. The phone call could be made any time. I was making up a bunch of Crappy Crap!

What was my solution? Make up Happy Crap! I imagined my sons working together to get the list done, arriving home to a peaceful house, producing wonderful work to delight my clients, and having a great telephone conversation. My shoulders relaxed and I enjoyed the drive home.

Were the chores done when I got home? Some were and some weren't, but the boys were working together to finish the list. If I had arrived home thinking negative thoughts, I would probably have made things worse by starting an argument. Stopping the Crappy Crap thinking allowed me to be at peace and see what had been accomplished, expect the best, and continue to build my most important relationships.

Practice the 3 Steps to Happy Crap: identify the facts, acknowledge your assumptions, and fill in the blanks with Happy Crap. Know your life script. Use the 8 Happy Crap tools, in whatever combination or frequency needed. Put your Happy Crap plan into practice. Then, choose to make one positive assumption and then another and another to rewrite your life story a little bit each day. You will tip the balance to positive and unleash more and more of your positive assumption power. Happy Crap will be your story. It is my story and as they say, *I'm sticking to it!*

Thank You!

Thank you for taking the time to read this book and consider what is written. I am hopeful that you have found just want you need to begin or to continue your journey. I can't think of a better adventure than choosing how your life will be each day and I am so grateful to have your company on the this Happy Crap path.

There is so much we don't have control over. Even if we think we should, or desperately wish we did, we just don't. Your *thinking*, with some practice, *is in your control.* Crappy Crap thinking leads to unhappiness and struggle. Happy Crap thinking is the road to ease and happiness.

If you are going to make up crap — and we all do — make up Happy Crap to unleash your power of positive assumptions.

If you are going to make up crap – and we all do – make up Happy Crap to unleash your power of positive assumptions. I wish you prosperity, productivity, and most importantly, peace!

About the Author

Erika Oliver

Erika Oliver is a Positive Approach Coach and the author of *Three Good Things: Happiness Every Day, No Matter What!* and *Three Good Things: A Coloring Book for Everyone!* She lives in Michigan with her husband, two sons, and two cats.

As a recovering pessimist, Erika's journey to optimism has been full of surprises. Sometimes the road is bumpy and other times unbelievably smooth. Erika's mission is to help people be healthy and happy. She believes that today is the very best day, every day! Erika writes a popular e-newsletter available at www.erikaoliver.com and has written feature articles in *Nonprofit World* magazine and other periodicals.

When she is not coaching people or working with teams, you will find Erika with her family and friends. She loves the ocean, the Great Lakes, the mountains, and just about anywhere else in nature. Erika's best day ever includes family, friends, fun and food!

Erika's men: Mark, Erik and Evan Oliver
Beach Vacation, Summer 2010

Other Positive Approach Books by Erika Oliver

Three Good Things: Happiness Every Day, No Matter What! is a true story of how Erika and her husband changed their perspective and their lives. It will inspire you and give you a simple, practical activity to move quickly toward having all good days!

$12.95

Three Good Things: A Coloring Book for Everyone! allows your logical brain to rest and activates creativity and intuition. You do not have to be an artist or even color inside the lines to enjoy this book. Original art by Erika.

$6.50

Books are available in quantity at a discount
from the publisher.

Contact Erika before Crappy Crap thinking sets in!
She is available for speaking, positive team development,
and coaching.

For more information on Erika Oliver,
Positive Approach Coach, inspiring people to
be healthy and happy, visit:

www.erikaoliver.com
(269) 760-6325